Wordsworth's Poetry of the Imagination

Wordsworth's Poetry of the Imagination

Charles Sherry

CLARENDON PRESS . OXFORD
1980

Oxford University Press, Walton Street, Oxford OX2 6DP

OXFORD LONDON GLASGOW
NEW YORK TORONTO MELBOURNE WELLINGTON
KUALA LUMPUR SINGAPORE JAKARTA HONG KONG TOKYO
DELHI BOMBAY CALCUTTA MADRAS KARACHI
NAIROBI DAR ES SALAAM CAPE TOWN

*Published in the United States
by Oxford University Press, New York*

British Library Cataloguing in Publication Data

Sherry, Charles
    Wordsworth's poetry of the imagination.
    1. Wordsworth, William – Criticism and
    interpretation
    I. Title
    821'.7   PR5888   79–41804

    ISBN 0–19–812655–7

*Typeset by Gloucester Typesetting Co. Ltd
and Printed in Great Britain by
Billing & Sons Ltd., London, Guildford and Worcester*

For Love
to
Marion
and to
James and David

Every man's condition is a solution in hieroglyphic to those inquiries he would put. He acts it as life, before he apprehends it as truth.

Infancy is the perpetual Messiah, which comes into the arms of fallen men, and pleads with them to return to paradise.

EMERSON

Preface

WHEN I began to study Wordsworth intensively, it was without any intention of writing on him. I was drawn into his orbit by the 'Intimations Ode', which I had taught several times, each time in a different situation. As my intimacy with the Ode increased, my understanding of it proportionally decreased; the familiar became unintelligible. What was particularly puzzling for me was the relationship between the enormous, yet very fragile power of the soul of the child and the mind of the adult in the act of recollecting it. Recollection was, it seemed, a considerable power of the mind. Through recollection the 'philosophic mind' of the 'Intimations Ode' acquires its particular perspective. And in reading *The Prelude* and the poetry gathered by Wordsworth under the heading 'Poems of the Imagination' in his collected poems I discovered more complex lines of relationship between the act of recollection and the mind of the poet.

Recollection of the soul's immortal power is dependent in Wordsworth upon its absence; it must fade and be diminished before the soul can recognize its nature. Recollection is the act through which the soul achieves a conscious recognition of its proper, human destiny. Through the agency of this recollective recognition the sphere of the mind's imaginative activity is also articulated. The imagination is constituted through the act of recollection, and the interplay between recollection and imagination shapes the essential character of Wordsworth's poetry of the imagination. Imagination and recollection are interpreted here as acts of mind which repeat a primary act of mind called, by Socrates, anamnesis.

This study of Wordsworth is written in four chapters, each of which circles around the interplay of recollection and imagination from a different perspective. The first chapter serves to set out, more or less descriptively, the basic pattern of the relation of recollection to imagination which the other three interpret from points of view determined by the nature of Wordsworth's own deepest concerns in his poetry of the imagination: language, growing up, and the 'marriage' of the mind with the external universe.

Inevitably there will be some repetition, but I have attempted to keep it at a minimum, and what repetition remains is intended as incremental.

Without the work of other scholars on Wordsworth a book of this kind would be impossible. My debt to them is very large, and will be clear to anyone familiar with their work. I would like particularly to acknowledge my debt to the work done on Wordsworth by four scholars: D. G. James's *Scepticism and Poetry*; Paul de Man's 'Wordsworth und Hölderlin'; Geoffrey Hartman's *Wordsworth's Poetry 1787–1814*; and Kenneth Johnston's 'The Idiom of Vision'. Although in many ways my argument runs counter to their views at various points, their speculations on imagination and divinity encouraged me to pursue mine.

I would like here to acknowledge the help and encouragement of friends and former colleagues in the writing of this book. Their response to it during the various stages of its development gave me the necessary assurance to complete and publish it. My thanks go to Walter Reed, Warwick Wadlington, and Jack Farrell who read critically different chapters; to Mike Holquist and Sidney Monas who both gave me a place to read publicly from work in progress; to David and Sharon Wevill, Christopher Middleton, and Prentiss Moore who read the completed text with a friendly eye; and to Jonathan Wordsworth and Richard Macksey for their help and advice in many important decisions. I want also to thank the students in my seminar on Coleridge and Wordsworth for their attention to and discussion of the major themes of this book.

CHARLES SHERRY

Austin,
Texas

Contents

CHAPTER I

The Perpetual Messiah: Recollection as Redemption

So lebt das Tier *unhistorisch*: denn es geht auf in der Gegenwart, wie ein Zahl, ohne dass ein wunderlicher Bruch übrigbleibt, es weiss sich nicht zu verstellen, verbirgt nichts und erscheint in jedem Momente ganz und gar als das, was es ist, kann also gar nicht anders sein als ehrlich.

NIETZSCHE

[I]

THE best of recent Wordsworth criticism, and much of it is brilliant, seems to have taken as the measure of its excellence its ability to interpret his poetry of the imagination. The difficulty in interpreting this poetry lies in determining precisely what happens when a 'visitation' of the imagination occurs. Most critics are agreed that a revelation or disclosure of what is divine, infinite, and immortal takes place in, or around, these visitations. But there is little or no agreement as to the locus of this revelation, the nature of its significance for Wordsworth, or the nature of the link between the poet and what is revealed to him.

Geoffrey Hartman has given these visitations an apocalyptic locus within a heightened form of consciousness toward which the poet feels himself drawn, only to withdraw upon coming near to it. Imagination, he says, reveals itself to the poet as a blinding power which leads him, by a *via naturaliter negativa*, beyond nature into the mind now aware of its increased power, and toward the defeat of poetry.

Wordsworth's experience, like Petrarch's or Augustine's, is a conversion: a turning about of the mind as from one belief to its opposite, and a turning *ad se ipsum*. It is linked to the birth of a sharper self-awareness, and accompanied by apocalyptic feelings. By 'apocalyptic' I mean there is an inner necessity to cast out nature, to extirpate everything apparently external to salvation, everything that might stand between the naked self and God, whatever risk in this to the self.[1]

Yet the 'apocalyptic risk' is one before which Wordsworth hesitates. The ascent of Snowdon is, Hartman says, 'Wordsworth's most astonishing avoidance of apocalypse'.[2] Imagination, like Heidegger's *Seyn*, in revealing itself in the landscape which opens out before the poet at the end of his ascent, remains concealed from him and 'cannot be localized in mind or nature or any part of nature'.[3] It is a moment in which consciousness, confronted by the might of its own powers, retreats from their presence by concealing from itself their source. By such concealment, such 'avoidance', poetry becomes possible. This interplay between revelation and concealment is reflected in the movement of Wordsworth's verse as it progresses toward and then away from the threatening revelation of the mind's power. It determines the structure of the mind's relation to nature and to its own past.

Caught up in the interplay of revelation and concealment, the mind floats, as it were, before nature searching for means to bind itself to natural objects through the creative act. Hartman shares with David Perkins[4] a sense of Wordsworth's creative mind as trapped within its own abyss and seeking a way out. The apocalyptic locus is, finally, nowhere but in the process of revelation and concealment which is the fundamental act of the poet's creative mind. Hartman is the 'phenomenological' interpreter of that process, and is bound by the horizon of approach and avoidance which he has discovered. His interpretation of Wordsworth's poetry is a descriptive rendering of the intricate manifestations of tha t process and a disclosure of the boundaries of its horizon.

In a brilliant essay, 'The Idiom of Vision',[5] Kenneth R. Johnston reverses the tendency of Hartman's interpretation to move away from the poem toward its origin in an apocalyptic locus within consciousness, while remaining for the most part within

---

[1] Geoffrey H. Hartman, *Wordsworth's Poetry 1787–1814* (New Haven and London, 1971), p. 49.

[2] Ibid., p. 61.

[3] Ibid., p. 65.

[4] David Perkins, *The Quest for Permanence: The Symbolism of Wordsworth Shelley and Keats* (Cambridge, 1959), pp. 24–6.

[5] Kenneth R. Johnston, 'The Idiom of Vision', in *New Perspectives on Coleridge and Wordsworth*, ed. Geoffrey H. Hartman (New York and London, 1972).

Hartman's conceptual horizon. Johnston does this by locating within a poem, Wordsworth's 'A Night-Piece', the point at which something visionary has taken place. This vision is something seen whose meaning is implicit in the process by which it is described.[6] Wordsworth's poems 'are the enactment or creation of a faith, not simply the expression of it'.[7] The faith which Wordsworth enacts in the poem inheres in nature and in the *excursive* power of the imagination to go out and meet it.[8] In such a visionary, excursive poetry the phenomena of nature are seen as embedded in apocalyptic structures. The language of the poem, its idiom, is the descriptive enactment of what is seen as visionary.

Johnston follows half of Hartman's thesis, he says, in agreeing that Wordsworth seeks to avoid apocalypse in 'A Night-Piece', but is unwilling to make fear of apocalypse the motive for that avoidance. Wordsworth avoids apocalypse, Johnston implies, because the vision in the poem is conjunctive.[9] Heaven and earth are brought together in man: 'The two spheres are brought together not so much by, as in, man; recognizing this mediate position, he defines his being'.[10] A man discovers himself as a midway point between heaven and earth, where mind and nature are seen as appropriately fitted to each other, yet distinct from one another. The vision is 'simultaneously disjunctive and conjunctive'.[11]

But as if to reaffirm an aspect of Hartman's thesis which he does not emphasize (that the imagination remains concealed as the condition of poetry), Johnston's interpretation rests upon the excursive power of the imagination to go out and meet nature, to embed, to use his language, the phenomenal processes of nature in an apocalyptic structure. What is seen, the vision embedded in the idiom of Wordsworth's poem, becomes the place where the mediate position of man is discovered by the poet. The poet's strikingly visual experience of nature in 'A Night-Piece' absorbs Johnston's interpretation, and the divine character of the power of the imagination is elided by it: the ground of the imagination's relation to the divine and infinite remains obscured and we see the imagination only as a shaping, excursive power acting in con-

---

6 Ibid., p. 5.   7 Ibid., p. 7.
8 Ibid., p. 8.   9 Ibid., p. 24.
10 Ibid.   11 Ibid., p. 25.

junction with nature. Although much that is of enormous significance has been said in Johnston's essay, we are left with the question it asked in the beginning: How does this vision happen? The vision in 'A Night-Piece' does not come from either nature alone, or from the isolated mind of man, or from the divine revealing itself to man, but from the conjunction of these. But upon what ground is that conjunction possible? The poem is the enactment of a faith in the conjunction of mind, nature, and the divine, yet the basis of that faith is not merely in what is seen, but in the significance of the way it is seen. What is the ground of that significance? It is not the poem itself, which is only the enactment of it. It lies in the particular capacity of the imagination to participate in both the divine and in nature, and by such participation to unite them in man. The excursive transcendence of the imagination toward nature and toward the divine has its ground in the mind of the poet. Transcendence toward nature and the divine as an ultimate totality happens in the act of imagination. How are we to understand the nature of this transcendence? It is the nature of this act which I wish to explore, to discover the meaning it has for the interpretation of Wordsworth's poetry.

The criticism of Hartman and Johnston raises several problems in the interpretation of Wordsworth which do not admit of an easy resolution. Johnston, within the visual limits to vision he has set, is able to locate the point in 'A Night-Piece' at which the visionary occurs, and by making man the place 'in' which the vision of heaven and earth is disjunctively conjoined he is able to circumscribe what is visionary within it. But the act of perception tells us nothing of the underlying reason why a thing is perceived as visionary or not. What is conjunctive *in* such an act of perception? Upon what basis or ground can this conjunction, in vision, of heaven and earth become intelligible? This is to ask the question concerning the nature of the relationship of the divine to the mortal, the infinite to the finite, and the One to the Many in Wordsworth's poetry of the imagination. It is a metaphysical question and as such is linked intimately with the processes of poetic creation. The analysis of that metaphysic will, I think, open it up as the ground and source of the poetry of the imagination,[12]

---

[12] The model I have in mind is Heidegger's 'destructive' reading of Kant in *Kant und das Problem der Metaphysik*. It is the speaking of what is not spoken in a text. See also the early chapters of *Sein und Zeit*.

in so far as, that is, it is the ground from which the poet's vision of the conjunction of heaven and earth arises.

There is a structure inherent in Wordworth's visionary experience, reflected, as Johnston has shown, in the idiom of his verse, whose ground and meaning remain obscured to the degree that the nature of the imagination itself remains concealed. To say, on the one hand, that the essential character of imaginative vision is to be found in the conjunction of heaven and earth discovered in it is an important accomplishment of contemporary interpretation; but on the other hand, to remain within the limits of such an interpretation is to restrict oneself to the conception of the imagination as an excursive power linking man to nature. In the sheer going out of imagination towards nature, its relation to the divine and infinite is obscured at its very basis. For why should this power to form a link between man and nature be considered divine, and not, as seems more likely, merely a 'power' of consciousness (raised to a heightened pitch)?

Consciousness alone, as Wordsworth repeatedly made clear,[13] is finite and perceives the world in a fragmentary manner. Such perception, in its extreme moments, forms the basis of a terrifying vision of a 'universe of death', a world in which nothing lives because all things are seen as isolated from one another. From such a universe the vivifying awareness of an 'under-sense',[14] the intuition or intimation of the totality to which they belong, is absent. It is what is divine in the imagination which makes possible the disclosure of the relation of the two spheres of heaven and earth to one another. The transcendent link of the finite to the infinite is revealed in the visitations of the imagination. But upon what basis? The revelation of the infinite in the finite in Wordsworth's poetry does not come from without, but is seen as coming from within. The imagination is an 'endowment'[15] of a mind standing in a privileged relation to its world.

Only in flashes, in privileged moments, is the finite world disclosed as a totality unified by its participation in what is intimated

[13] See for example, *The Prelude* (1805), VII, 695–740. Unless otherwise specified all other quotations from *The Prelude* will be from the 1805 version, ed. Ernest de Selincourt (London, 1947).

[14] *Prelude*, VII, 711.

[15] *The Excursion*, I, 77–80, in *The Poetical Works of William Wordsworth*, vol.v, ed. Ernest de Selincourt and Helen Darbishire (Oxford, 1959). Hereafter *The Poetical Works* will be cited as *PW*.

as divine and whole. The earth without these moments of illumi-
nation is 'blind'.[16] There is nothing in nature, in man, or in the
cities of men from which the presence of the divine may be
intuited without the intervenient occurrence of the visitations of
the imagination. Revelation is not continual. In Book VI of *The
Prelude* nature is read as a book of apocalyptic symbols, but the
prior condition for such reading (which transforms the discrete
objects of nature into a legible text) is the visitation of the
imagination occurring upon Wordworth's discovery that he had,
without realizing it, crossed over the Alps. This discovery is
experienced as a displacement from his accustomed and habitual
relationship to nature. During such moments of displacement the
imagination emerges and occupies, as a powerful, disruptive force,
the displaced bond between the poet and the natural world.

The disclosure of the link between the divine and the mortal
does not proceed through the agency of some external force, but
is recognized as an endowment of the poet's mind. In this study I
wish to explore the hypothesis that the source of the imagination
and of what is divine in its visitations is the child's anamnestic
view of the world as it is represented in the 'Intimations Ode' and
in Wordsworth's commentary upon it in the Fenwick note to that
poem. The link between the divine and the mortal rests upon the
child's mortal/immortal vision of the natural world before the
'Shades of the prison-house' begin closing down around it. The
significance of the way in which the child regards the world is
only discovered in recollection, after that vision has been largely
lost. It is for the man looking back at his experience of the world
as a child that the anamnestic vision of nature takes on a meaning
it could never have had for the child. For the man looking back in
recollection, this vision becomes an intimation of the divine origin
of the soul and a promise that the end of life will be a return to
that origin. The 'Intimations Ode' is founded upon the conscious
recollection of an unconscious memory. Recollection is the act
which recovers, by raising it into consciousness, the significance
of the child's unconscious remembrance of how it once perceived
the presence of the divine. For Wordsworth, as for Socrates,[17]
anamnesis is a form of remembrance enabling man to perceive

---

[16] See *The Excursion*, VI, 256–8.

[17] The most important of the Socratic dialogues in this respect are *Phaedrus, Phaedo, Meno,* and *Philebus.* In *Phaedrus* the metaphors of the prison-house and the dimming

certain permanent, even eternal, truths once he remembers to remember them, and through their recollection raise them once again to conscious significance. What the child retains anamnesti- cally remains unconscious so long as the child remains unaware of the division between itself and the natural world, unaware of its own mortality, and oblivious of the distinction between the objective world and its own subjective existence. Once the child reaches the point where it is able to grasp as real the difference between itself and the natural world, in the awareness of its own mortality, then the conditions emerge which make possible the recollection of what had been forgotten and the discovery through that recollection of the significance of the child's anamnestic vision.

The world the child sees in the 'Intimations Ode' is characterized by 'fallings from us, vanishings'. Wordsworth tells us in the Fenwick note[18] that as a child he had occasionally to reach out to grasp things to reassure himself of their reality, and that accompanying these sensations of instability was an inability to grasp his own mortality (he felt, he said, that he would not die, but would be transported to heaven like Elijah). Those moments when the imagination is present for the poet are triggered by an experience of the natural world which repeats Wordsworth's childhood perception of things: his world falls away from him, and vanishes. Almost every one of the privileged moments where the imagination emerges is preceded by an incident in which, as in the crossing of the Simplon Pass, the poet discovers the natural world to be *other* than it had seemed to be. The poet reaches out, as it were, to grasp the world and discovers it, in that act, to be

---

of vision which occurs when the soul falls into a body are to be found. I consider them to be analogues and not sources for Wordsworth. *Phaedo* (75e) contains the following passage, whose importance is clear: 'And if it is true that we acquired our knowledge before our birth, and lost it at the moment of birth, but afterward, by the exercise of our senses upon sensible objects, recover the knowledge which we had once before, I suppose that what we call learning will be the recovery of our own knowledge, and surely we should be right in calling this recollection.' (from *The Collected Dialogues of Plato*, ed. Edith Hamilton and Huntington Cairns, trans. Hugh Tredennick (New York, 1963), p. 59). In *Meno* Socrates speculates on the truth, which comes from Pindar among other sources, that the soul is immortal, through a demonstration of a slave's capacity for working out geometrical problems. And in the *Philebus* he makes an important distinction between memory, as the retention of sensation, and recollection, which is the *recapturing by and in the soul* of what the soul and body experienced together.

18 *PW*, vol. IV, pp. 463–5, and 467.

quite unlike what it seemed to be. In the momentary displacement
of the poet's intimate and habitual bond with the natural world
the imagination emerges as the repetition of his earlier anamnestic
perception of the world.

The origin of the poetry of the imagination is the repetition for
the poet, now grown, of his anamnestic perception of the world
as a child. It is a repetition with a difference, however, for the child
senses no meaning in what it perceives as what is simply present
for it. For the poet the significance of the child's vision, experi-
enced in its repetition, lies in the disclosure made through that
repetition of the relation of the finite to the infinite. This relation-
ship is not immediately disclosed, but is implicit in the experience
of the visitation of the imagination. It is not raised to conscious
significance until it is recollected, 'as a thing divine', by the poet.
Recollection, seen in relation to the experience of the visitation
of the imagination, becomes the repetition of a repetition of an
originary experience, and by such repetition recollection raises
that experience to conscious significance as the basis of the poet's
vision of the link between the divine and the mortal.

Recollection is the discovery of the significance of what is
revealed in the visitation of the imagination. It is the act which
tethers or binds that revelation, as something divine, to the world
of the poet. The poet's discovery of the meaning of what has been
revealed to him constitutes what remains of the visionary experi-
ence after it has passed. Socrates speaks in the *Meno* (98a) about
the necessity of recollecting those ultimate truths we know
anamnestically. They are like Daedalus' statues, he says, which
will slip away from their owners unless they are tethered. Recollec-
tion is the fashioning of those tethers, whereby we discover the
reasons by which we retain ultimate truths. For Wordsworth,
recollection serves a similar purpose. In the discovery, through
recollection, of the significance of what he has seen in the visita-
tions of the imagination, he binds that vision to himself as the
intimation of something divine. Recollection is a tethering of those
fundamental truths which are essential to the growth of the poet,
to his ability to progress in stages through life, a life seen not
merely as the steady diminishment of his divine light, but as the
gathering together of what it has illumined.

The pattern inherent in the poet's experience—displacement,
visitation of the imagination as anamnestic repetition, and recol-

lection—is the originary form of the poetry of the imagination. In the following fragment from the 'Christabel' notebook, recollection, as the activity through which the recovery of the significance of the moment when the 'light of sense goes out', is articulated:

> In many a walk
> At evening or by moonlight, or reclined
> At midday upon beds of forest moss,
> Have we to Nature and her impulses
> Of our whole being made free gift, and when
> Our trance had left us, oft have we, by aid
> Of the impressions which it left behind,
> Looked inward on ourselves, and learned, perhaps,
> Something of what we are.[19]
>
> (vi, 8–16)

This pattern, where recollection turns inward to disclose the significance of an experience which would otherwise remain concealed, is embedded in its totality in many of the poems of the imagination, and is to be partially seen in all of them. It is not only a visual pattern inherent in the visionary experiences of the poet and reflected in the idiom of his poetry, but it is also the fundamental form of disclosure lying at the origin of his imaginative poems and as such it determines the form and character of the poetry happening through it. What is revealed in the visitation of the imagination and disclosed through recollection of it determines the form of that poetry. Such disclosure is grounded in an interplay of concealment and revelation.[20] In the first instance, the finite, fragmentary, 'blind' world is revealed as a participant in a divine totality hidden from a finite, temporally blinded consciousness. In the second, what is disclosed in the recollection of the visitation of the imagination as the participation of that finite consciousness in a divine totality, is itself never fully manifested, but present only as an *intimation* of a greater, even infinite power of the mind.

In this first chapter I want to make the outlines of this pattern

---

[19] *PW*, vol. v, pp. 343–4.
[20] Two essays of Heidegger are essential for understanding the interplay between concealment and disclosure in his thought: 'Vom Wesen der Wahrheit', and 'Der Ursprung des Kunstwerkes'.

inherent in Wordsworth's poetry of the imagination more complete through an interpretation of two related poems, 'Beggars' and 'Sequel to the Foregoing', and by a partial interpretation of the 'Intimations Ode' which will limn in the dimensions of the problematic linking of imagination with anamnesis. My interpretation of the great Ode will be partial in this first chapter because I am taking it as a paradigm for all of Wordsworth's poetry of the imagination. Though it is not included among the poems of the imagination in the final edition of his works, I regard it as the most complete, and the most difficult, of all his imaginative poems. I shall recur to it throughout the various stages of this study, the aim of which is to explore speculatively the implications of the relationship between imagination and anamnesis for the interpretation of Wordsworth's imaginative poetry, and to see how we can understand the relation of mind to nature, the growth of the poet's mind, and the nature of his language, particularly metaphor, in the light of such speculative interpretation.

[II]

Repetition is a dominant pattern in Wordsworth's poetry. It acquires different forms of signification according to the mode and manner in which it is employed.[21] Wordsworth's 'Beggars' (composed 13–14 March 1802—published 1807) has its repetition in 'Sequel to the Foregoing', written some fifteen years later (composed 1817—published 1827).[22] In the final edition of Wordsworth's poetry these two poems are gathered together with the poems of the imagination. 'Beggars' is based upon an experience of Dorothy's which she related to the poet.[23] Wordsworth told Henry Crabb Robinson that he wrote the poem 'to exhibit the power of physical beauty and health and vigour in childhood, even in a state of moral depravity'.[24]

---

[21] Two critics have discussed at length, and with particular insight, the problem of interpreting repetition in Wordsworth's poetry: Herbert A. Lindenberger, *On Wordsworth's 'Prelude'* (Princeton, 1963), and Frances C. Ferguson, 'The Lucy Poems: Wordsworth's Quest for a Poetic Object', *English Literary History (ELH)*, vol. XL, No. 4, 1973, pp. 532–48.

[22] The dating of these poems is that of Ernest de Selincourt, *PW*, vol.II.

[23] See de Selincourt's note on 'Beggars' in *PW*, vol. II, pp. 508–9.

[24] Henry Crabb Robinson, *Diary, Reminiscences, and Correspondence*, vol. I, selected and edited by Thomas Sadler (London and New York, 1872), p. 139.

'Beggars' is the relation of the poet's encounter with a tall and majestic beggar woman (with hints of the gypsy in her appearance) to whom he gives alms. He continues on his way only to confront a short distance ahead two young boys chasing after butterflies in a field. The poet perceives a distinct resemblance between the boys and the woman he has just met; yet, when the boys accost him, begging in 'a plaintive whine', and he tells them he has just given something to their mother, they tell him, in turn, they have no mother, that she is long dead. The poet refuses to believe then, and they, indifferent to his refusal, run back to their play.

The 'Sequel to the Foregoing' seems to begin from the mood induced by the question asked in its opening line, 'Where are they now, those wanton Boys?' The poet asks, after many years have elapsed, 'but all is dark between!' He does not, and cannot, know what has happened to them. But the asking about their fate, even when such asking is consciously in vain, opens up a dark space which can be illumined by the projection of a belief that nothing truly harmful has come to them:

> Kind Spirits! may we not believe
> That they, so happy and so fair
> Through your sweet influence, and the care
> Of pitying Heaven, at least were free
> From touch of *deadly* injury?
> Destined, whate'er their earthly doom,
> For mercy and immortal bloom?
>
> (36–42)

Such a belief is not grounded in the logic of everyday, matter-of-fact events, but in the 'genial hour' in which the poet saw them 'Walk through the fire with unsinged hair' like youthful creatures from an Old Testament story.[25] It is the remembrance of this 'genial hour' which becomes the impetus and heart of the poem. Understood in this regard, the poem can be seen as an attempt to articulate the validity, the reality, and the constancy of what was revealed to the poet in that hour. It is an exhibition of 'the power of physical beauty and health and vigour in childhood', which

---

[25] There is a similar line in *The Prelude*, VII, 397–8, referring to a young boy the poet saw in the crowd at a London theatre: 'Like one of those who walk'd with hair unsinged/Amid the fiery furnace'.

manifests the *power* of the poet to see and exhibit a power which would otherwise not have been seen. The 'Sequel' repeats the theme of the 'Beggars' in order to reaffirm it as a faith and a belief. But what was there in the first poem to put into question the vision of that 'genial hour'? What remains unaffirmed and unspoken in 'Beggars' that would require or elicit the repetition of the 'Sequel' to raise it to a conscious presence?

It is the difference in 'Beggars' between what seems to be the case in the poet's vision of the two boys at play and what is (really) there. The difference between what they seem to be and what they are is the creative matrix of both poems. In the first poem, seen from the perspective of the second, it seems as though the 'genial hour' was the producer of the illusion that the little boys 'seemed fit/For finest tasks of earth or air'. This is a deception, as the poet immediately discovers on coming closer to the boys and discovering in their plaintive whine that, though they *seem* different from the mother, in fact they are not. The initial discrepancy between the mother and the children, and subsequently between what the children seem to be and what they are constitutes the creative matrix of the poem.

The 'Sequel' is a poem of much less intensity, and is much flatter and more direct in stating its meaning, as so much of Wordsworth's later poetry is. It is a reaffirmation through remembrance of a belief in what was seen in years past. Even though the poet's faith in what he has seen in a genial hour might be deceptive, it need not be, and need not destroy the capacity of the poet to believe in the power of what he has seen. 'Beggars' seemed to put into question the validity of what the poet saw, and by extension the validity of his capacity to see (in a visionary sense). In the act of recollection which constitutes the temporal unity of the 'Sequal', a belief in what was vouchsafed in a 'genial hour' many years ago is reaffirmed in the hope that what the poet saw of beauty and grace in those wanton children was able to keep them from 'deadly' harm. It is a reaffirmation which can be neither totally confirmed nor absolutely denied. Such confirmation is not possible because the requisite proof is absent, but its very absence, 'all is dark between', allows for the presence of hope, and for the affirmation, however partial, of what was granted to the poet at that moment. What the poet reaffirms, along with his faith that no serious harm has come to the children, is his trust in the genial hour, in its power, when what he saw was vouchsafed to him with the certainty of vision. In 'A Sequal' the poet speaks what was not spoken in 'Beggars' and reaffirms the validity of the vision of that genial hour. What he did not say in 'Beggars' is that those boys 'walked through fire'.

The implications of the repetition in 'A Sequal' of what was spoken in 'Beggars', and its location within a displacement occurring between what the poet saw in a genial moment and what he discovers in fact to be there are important to the interpretation of Wordsworth's poetry of the imagination. This displacement is an event whose significance is given and disclosed in its recollection. The meaning of that encounter as a moment when the imagination was present to the poet, enabling him to see the children in relation to their participation in the divine and immortal fire, is itself made present only through the recollection of that moment. Imagination and recollection are linked together as event and interpretation. The presence of the imagination is discovered in the displacement of the poet's vision, where the poet finds that his perception of the essential qualities of the natural world has failed him in an important way. That experience of the genial hour is undergone as an immediate usurpation of the poet's habitual perception of nature, as a denial of what he seems to discover in the boys' plaintive whine. It is an experience whose significance is not clear in 'Beggars'. In recollecting it in 'A Sequel', the poet discovers its significance as a visitation of the imagination, as a moment when the mortal, finite, and fragmentary are seen in their permanent, yet hidden, relation to the immortal, infinite, and One: a totality which embraces heaven and earth and sustains them in their being.

There is no point where this totality is ever clearly and imaginatively revealed to Wordsworth. It is opened to him at intervenient moments in his life, moments which are intimations, not direct revelations, of a divine totality. They are intimations which do not come from outside, but from within and have their origin in moments when the 'light of sense' fails him, as it did in his vision of the two beggar boys, or in his failure to perceive the way in crossing the Simplon Pass. Such failure to see the natural world is a displacement of the bond of intimate and loving perception of nature which has its origin in the mother's love for her child.[26]

[26] As in *The Prelude*, II, 240–5:

    . . . the Babe who Sleeps

When that bond is displaced that other form of the perception of the world which belongs to the child emerges with the force of a power long suppressed. In the Fenwick note to the 'Intimations Ode' Wordsworth describes his perception of the external world when he was a child in this way: '. . . I was often unable to think of external things as having external existence, and I communed with all that I saw as something not apart from, but inherent in, my own immaterial nature.'[27] It is a mode of perception, divine in origin, and compelled to view its world through a mortal eye. The world seen thus appears under an anamnestic shadow. Things fall away. The world is not seen by the light of common day, but in the light of heaven shining through the child's eyes.

When the 'light of sense' fails him at crucial moments the world appears to Wordsworth once again under its anamnestic shadow, as a place seen through the child's recollection of its heavenly home. Anamnesis is a knowledge of the world derived from the soul's recollection of how it saw the presence of the divine. In Wordsworth the child's anamnestic perception of nature becomes the ground from which spring the visitations of the imagination, those moments when the world is seen once again in its relation to the divine and infinite. This link between imagination and anamnesis becomes clearer in Wordsworth's 'Intimations Ode' and the Fenwick note to it.

[III]

The interpreter of Wordsworth's 'Intimations Ode' confronts in the poet's awareness of death an old philosophical problem: the degeneration of the One into the Many.[28] It is what Plotinus in

---

        Upon his Mother's breast, who, when his soul
        Claims manifest kindred with an earthly soul,
        Doth gather passion from his Mother's eye!
        Such feelings pass into his torpid life
        Like an awakening breeze, . . .

[27] *PW*, vol. v, loc. cit.

[28] During the Romantic period this problem was revived in both its traditional Neoplatonic formulations, through Coleridge for one, and in its post-Kantian transformations, through Schiller, Hegel, Hölderlin, Schelling, and their contemporaries. In its several variations the relationship of the One to the Many was one of the great problems of the time. Schiller's famous distinction between naive and sentimental poetry rests upon it; Hölderlin's *Hyperion* is built around it; Coleridge's definition of the esemplastic power of the primary imagination is a direct expression of it.

the Third Ennead called Eternity's clothing itself with time. In the Fenwick note to the 'Immortality Ode' Wordsworth said that the 'fall of man presents an analogy' in favour of the argument of that poem. Otherwise construed, the fall of the One into the Many is the immortal child's discovery of its mortal finitude. The Ode begins with that discovery. The poet sees that he stands outside nature, outside the harmonious, unbroken totality of the child's life as a creature in nature. Not death, but the awareness of death separates the man from the child. All things in nature must die; only man possesses the awareness of death's certainty. In that awareness of death lies his finitude, his sense that his existence is bounded by his coming hither and his going hence. This consciousness of his beginning and end separates him from the natural, sensuous unity of the natural world. The poet, now grown, has fallen out of nature and despairs of ever returning to it. Life is not one any more, but many. The sensuous unity of the child's life in nature has degenerated into the finite, repetitive, discontinuous world of the adult:

> As if his whole vocation
> Were endless imitation.

Death is universal; but only man lives in a 'universe of death'. Within it, death signifies. What it signifies alters in the 'Intimations Ode'. From the perspective first presented in the poem, death seems to be the absolute end of everything. Beyond it there is nothing visible. For the poet, conscious only of his finitude, death is not a part of anything, but the end point whose discovery fragments life. Death is the point which, once discovered, repeats itself in life, transforming the natural harmony of things into a discontinuous series of points. These stations on life's way, each as discrete and meaningless as death itself, become empty repetitions of roles 'conned' by an actor condemned to play them out. The poet's awareness of death has fragmented the organic unity of his life. The poet longs to escape from this scattering of his life's inner continuity. But if he is to do so the significance of death must alter for him.

The poet does not know how he fell out of nature. He possesses only the awareness that he is no longer a part of it. And that awareness is presented as a question which remains unanswered:

'Whither is fled the visionary gleam?' The Ode begins with a dis-
covery of this fall, but it ends in the alteration of the conditions
surrounding it. Somehow the poet has put the fragmented world
generated in the awareness of death behind him. Death's signifi-
cance has altered. No longer an absolute end, death has become
visible as a part once more of a totality accessible to the poet. The
precise nature of that totality remains ambiguous and undefined.
What is certain is the poet's intuition of it and of the power of that
intuition to alter the significance of death. In this inner trans-
formation, life's meaning changes too. No longer a series of dis-
crete roles, life assumes an inner continuity once again. The
spontaneous happiness of the child becomes the reflective, sombre
aspiration of the grown man. In the movement originating in the
poet's transformed awareness of death the despair of a life con-
demned to endless repetitions is transcended.

It is the intimation of a totality embracing life and death as
elements of its continuity, not the immediately apprehended pre-
sence of such a unity, which makes this transcendence possible.
This totality encompasses the natural world, but lies beyond it as
well. Nature is a part of it, and death for both man and natural
creatures is also a part of it. The poet's knowledge of this totality
does not come from his intuition of nature alone. It is not always
visible there. His knowledge comes, rather, from his experience
of nature as a child.

The poet's access to this totality, this divine presence in the
world, lies in his recollecting the child's perception of things in
nature as it first came into the world:

> Not for these I raise
> The song of thanks and praise;
> But for those obstinate questionings
> Of sense and outward things,
> Fallings from us, vanishings;

In the world, but not of it yet, the child remains unaware of the
significance inherent in the peculiarities of its perception of
things. The recollection of the poet discloses the significance of
those peculiarities and finds in them the presence of a totality
encompassing and transcending the natural world. In memory the
poet is able to repeat the experience of the child's groping per-

ception of things in nature. This repetition in memory discloses
the significance of that perception. The child is not aware of that
significance. Only the experience of the infinite in its relation to
the finite world is his. Recollection discloses the meaning of that
experience. That is anamnesis' particular power for Wordsworth.
In the 'Intimations Ode' the image of the child playing on the
shore of the sea is the figure of man's relationship to the infinite.
It is also in its variations which include shepherds, reapers, and
hermits seen in lordly isolation against the firmament, the figure
of the poet's experience of the imagination's 'visitations'. The
meaning of these visitations is also disclosed through the act of
recollection.

Memory must have, then, a particular power for Wordsworth,
something beyond the early formulation of 'emotion recollected
in tranquillity'. In the activity of recollection the way out of a
fragmented world is discovered. Although the child remains
oblivious to the meaning of its anamnestic vision, the poet dis-
covers its meaning in the act of recollection. His gaze turns back-
wards over the course he has travelled inland away from the im-
mortal sea and comes to rest upon the child playing on the shore.
It is an act whose essence is distance and repetition. Distance
separates the poet from his early experience of the world and
frees him for the discovery of its significance. And repetition
brings that experience near once again, not in its original form,
but as an experience whose meaning has been disclosed and now
accompanies it. For the man, now become a poet, the activity of
recollection, by disclosing their significance, discovers both the
configuration of the child's anamnestic vision of nature, and what
the visitations of the imagination reveal. In the interpretive inter-
dependence of childhood vision and anamnesis, and anamnesis
and imagination the possibilities exist for reading the things of
the natural world as figures of the 'Apocalypse', and not as the
gloomy wardens of a prison-house or the meaningless pieces of a
fragmented world. The interpretation of the 'Intimations Ode'
depends, then, upon understanding that interdependence, upon
seeing how through it the Many are disclosed in their relation-
ship to the One. The poetry of the imagination is the revelation
of that hidden relationship.

The figure Wordsworth uses to embody the relationship
between anamnesis and childhood vision in the 'Intimations Ode',

and between anamnesis and imagination in *The Prelude*, is that of two consciousnesses belonging to the poet at different periods of his life. The link between them is memory. One consciousness is the poet's as he writes, and the other was once his earlier in his life. The earlier one is separate from the later, and is present to it only in recollection. What the earlier consciousness only vaguely felt and apprehended as a sensuous confusion of sound, motion, and light stands disclosed in its essential configurations by the act of recollection belonging to the later consciousness. The immediate moment was always an unstable one for Wordsworth. What he experienced in that moment was dimly apprehended and feebly grasped. But in recollecting it he was able to discover in the confusion of his sensations an order not immediately visible. This is especially true of those moments of the imagination's visitations when the natural world stood revealed in its relation to the totality which sustained and governed it; when the finite world, that is, was seen in its relation to the infinite and divine power encompassing it. In the recollection of such moments nature became a language he could read and a voice he could hear. The world of the child in the 'Intimations Ode' is essentially identical to the world as it appears in the visitations of the imagination. As the intimacy of the child's intercourse with the presence of the eternal in nature begins to grow more distant, the act of recollection begins to supplant the role of immediate perception. In recollection the meaning of the child's experience of nature is discovered. Recollection becomes for the man now grown the source of his knowledge as to his place on earth and of his destiny after death. The man travels from an unconscious intimacy with the eternal presence toward an awareness of the significance of that intimacy. Through anamnesis the meaning of the world's relation to the divine is given, and the eternal presence discovered in the child's vision of nature is recognized as the home from which the soul has come and toward which it is progressing. In such recognition lies the constitution of the poet's faith that 'look through death'. In such recollection the life of the soul is intuited as a whole, as belonging to a totality which encompasses both its life on earth and its destiny after death. The child standing alone, gazing into eternity, like one of Wordsworth's shepherds, is the image of the poet in his special relation, through the imagination, to that totality. In recollection, the child sporting on the shore of the immortal sea is also the figure upon which the philosophic mind is founded.

Each man, Wordsworth says, is a 'memory to himself', a single point of recollection where finite and infinite, mortal and immortal are joined:

> O Heavens! how awful is the might of Souls,
> And what they do within themselves, while yet
> The yoke of earth is new to them, the world
> Nothing but a wild field where they were sown.
> This is, in truth, heroic argument,
> And genuine prowess; which I wish'd to touch
> With hand however weak; but in the main
> It lies far hidden from the reach of words.
> Points have we all of us within our souls,
> Where all stand single; this J feel, and make
> Breathings for incommunicable powers,
> Yet each man is a memory to himself,
> And, therefore, now that I must quit this theme,
> I am not heartless; for there's not a man
> That lives who hath not had his godlike hours,
> And knows not what majestic sway we have,
> As natural beings in the strength of nature.
>
> (*Prelude*, III, 178–94)

To 'stand single' is to stand alone in the presence of things seen as a unified and single totality. In this passage from *The Prelude* the dominant themes of the 'Intimations Ode' are obliquely stated: the soul's discovery of its finitude and singleness in its earthly life, and the relation of anamnesis to the 'godlike' hours which every man has experienced. These themes constitute the 'heroic argument' of the 'Intimations Ode'. In recollection the path back towards the soul's origin stands revealed. Recollection retrieves the significance of the soul's early moments on earth. The journey of the soul through an earth alien to it has its beginning in the discovery of its singleness, its finitude, and its fallenness. The soul, Wordsworth says, is sown in a 'wild field' where there are no clear markings of its origin or of its purpose. These cannot be discovered in the earth or in the cities which man has built upon it. On the other hand, life is clearly regarded as a journey in the 'Intimations Ode'. But in this passage from *The Prelude* there is no mention of it. For movement to become a journey it must have a beginning and an end however vaguely apprehended. No journey seems possible in the wild field of the earth. There is no sense of a beginning or of an end to be discovered in its confused appearance. There is only the yoke-like burden of the earth itself. Wordsworth indicates the influence over a man's life which his godlike hours may have, but does not take up the argument and complete it.

He does complete it in the 'Intimations Ode' when he discovers in recollection the meaning of his own godlike hours and finds in them the beginning and also the intimation of the end of his life. The force of recollection transforms the wild field of the earth into a pathway over which he journeys. It is a pathway whose markers and indicators he is able to read. The child follows this path unconsciously. The man conscious of his own mortality senses that there was a path for him once, but that he can no longer perceive it. But in recollection he recovers the way he had lost. The earth once again speaks to him and becomes a place for his journey to be made. For the child, 'unconscious intercourse' with the divine presence in nature remains without significance. He sees the figures of the 'Apocalypse' but does not understand that they constitute a language. It is a language which the grown man learns to read by recovering in recollection the significance of the child's unconscious intercourse with the divine.

In his intimate and loving familiarity with nature, the child feeds upon the presence of eternal beauty manifest in its radiant images. It is a relationship whose intimacy is patterned after the child's love for its mother, but whose prototype is the soul's relation to its divine source. Though the man stands single, aware that he is a stranger to a world he once delighted in, that happier world is not totally lost to him. In recollection he can recover the significance of that world manifest to the child in its immediate perception of things in nature.

Wordsworth discovered a number of analogies for expressing the relation of the finite to the divine, infinite totality encompassing it as it was revealed to him in his recollection of the visitations of the imagination. Many of these analogies come from St. Augustine: the intuition of the eternal moment, the idea of mystical union with the eternal, and the concept of *caritas* are all figures, taken from *The Confessions*, for the relation of the infinite to the finite. Wordsworth often echoes the language of St. John when referring to this relationship. Though he used the polymorphous language of Christian revelation, what Wordsworth meant by it was something quite different, whose significance derived from his own private experience of the divine in childhood. What remained constant for Wordsworth through all the variations of language was the fixed presence of recollection. It was the single point from which the world Wordsworth lived in was disclosed as united with the eternal and divine. It was a unique point, whose nature was for ever inexpressible, for which the poet could only make 'breathings', around which the figures of Christian revelation orbited.

The relationship of recollection to the visitations of the imagination (understood as anamnestic repetitions) in *The Prelude* is invaluable to the interpreter of the 'Intimations Ode' for what it says about the relationship of the childhood vision and anamnesis. What, precisely, is revealed in the visitations of the imagination? What is being said through the analogies which Wordsworth chose to express a unique experience? Wordsworth once told Crabb Robinson that he felt no need for a personal saviour. Perhaps the origin of that statement lies in his faith in the power of recollection to recover his relationship to the divine.

The visitation of the imagination is an event with three distinct moments. An overmastering usurpation of the outward senses is the first of these: the light of sense goes out. Accompanying it is a distinct sense that a boundary has been inadvertently crossed and that the poet stands in a new relationship to the world. Once the moment of usurpation is past, he sees the things of the world differently. This newly acquired perception of things constitutes the second moment. In it the revelation of a world invisible to the ordinary sense occurs. What Wordsworth called a 'great Nature' is discovered. For him, this 'great Nature' exists also in the visionary work of 'mighty' poets.[29] Such revelations are granted to some poets and constitute the difference between greater and lesser poets. In these revelations the speech of the world is recovered; the wild field in which man's soul was sown is transformed into a world of signs indicating the relationship of man to the infinite and divine totality which sustains his life. A chaotic, silent landscape is transformed by this revelation into a country where directions are given and a journey through it becomes

[29] The passage referred to here is *The Prelude*, V, 608–29.

possible. The lost traveller discovers his path once more. The confusion of life in the city is transfigured by the weight of its history and becomes an ordered cosmos. Recollection is the third moment which brings the other two to completion by discovering in them the significance they inherently bear, that is, that they were divine intimations. In recollection the revelation of man's relation to the infinite is repeated. The experience of the infinite in repetition is no longer something which overwhelms the senses, but becomes an event perceived through its accompanying signification.

These three moments are present in the 'Intimations Ode', and there, seen in their relation to the child's anamnestic vision, they are not as clearly distinct from one another as they are in *The Prelude*. The pattern of these moments in *The Prelude* repeats the relationship of the poet to his early anamnestic experiences as they are presented in the 'Intimations Ode'. The power of recollection to recover the significance of the experience of the infinite is more overtly represented in *The Prelude*. And it is the power of recollection which enables the poet to move beyond the fragmented perception of his life created by his awareness of death toward the 'philosophic mind' of the 'Intimations Ode'.

There are two passages in *The Prelude*, quite different from one another, where the pattern of which I have been speaking emerges with especial clarity: the young Wordsworth's first entry into London, and the more famous, and much discussed, passage describing the crossing of the Alps through the Simplon Pass.

There was a moment, Wordsworth says, during his journey to London when he knew that the threshold of the city had been overpassed: it was not clearly marked and only once it was overpassed did he know unknowingly that he was within the city. With the awareness that he has stepped over a boundary comes a sense, though vague, that 'high things' lie hidden in the dreary presence of the city:

> Never shall I forget the hour
> The moment rather say when having thridded
> The labyrinth of suburban Villages,
> At length I did unto myself first seem
> To enter the great City. On the roof
> Of an itinerant Vehicle I sate

With vulgar Men about me, vulgar forms
Of houses, pavement, streets, of men and things,
Mean shapes on every side: but, at the time,
When to myself it fairly might be said,
The very moment that I seem'd to know
The threshold now is overpass'd, Great God!
That aught *external* to the living mind
Should have such mighty sway! yet so it was
A weight of Ages did at once descend
Upon my heart; no thought embodied, no
Distinct remembrances; but weight and power,
Power growing with the weight: alas! I feel
That I am trifling: 'twas a moment's pause.
All that took place within me, came and went
As in a moment, and I only now
Remember that it was a thing divine.
                              (*Prelude*, VIII, 688–709)

London in one of its aspects was for Wordsworth a 'Parliament
of Monsters' (*Prelude*, VII, 691) whose image was accurately re-
flected in the monstrosities of motion, colour, shape, and sound
celebrating Saint Bartholomew's Fair. These monsters embody
everything that is terrible, trivial, and demeaning in the city. They
inhabit the universe of endless, empty repetition by which the
poet finds himself threatened at the beginning of the 'Intimations
Ode'. His condemnation of that life is almost total:

Oh blank confusion! and a type not false
Of what the mighty City is itself
To all except a Straggler here and there,
To the whole Swarm of its inhabitants;
An indistinguishable world to men,
The slaves unrespited of low pursuits,
Living amid the same perpetual flow
Of trivial objects, melted and reduced
To one identity, by differences
That have no law, no meaning, and no end;
Oppression under which even highest minds
Must labour, whence the strongest are not free;
                              (*Prelude*, VII, 695–706)

The city presents a confused and meaningless series of images
reduced to a single identity, which is really no identity at all.

Everything in it appears accidental and without purpose, incapable of being whole or seen as a whole. It is a world lacking any clear or visible markings of its significance. The confusion of a life without identity is immediately present to the poet, but concealed within the accidental, haphazard appearance it offers lies the 'weight of Ages' which produced it. It is the power of a history, as something quite other than the knowledge of it, which is revealed to the poet as he crosses the threshold of the city. This revelation of the weight and power of the history of the city transfigures its mean streets. No longer do they contain a jumble of senselessly confused objects. They are 'thronged with impregnations' (VIII, 790), alive with the historical power which made them. The revelation of this historical force transforms the transitory and accidental appearance of the city and makes it something stable and constant, whose power of endurance resembles that of nature itself. It is not knowledge (as Wordsworth seems to imply in the 1850 version of *The Prelude*), but the intimation of a tremendous historical force impregnating the city which is revealed to the poet. It is a revelation very much like the ones granted to him during his early life in the country. His perception of things in the city resembles his vision of nature, where the natural world is seen in its relation to the infinite totality sustaining it, and the city is perceived as impregnated with the tremendous, ungraspable power of its history.

> 'Tis true the History of my native Land,
> With those of Greece compar'd and popular Rome,
> Events not lovely nor magnanimous,
> But harsh and unaffecting in themselves
> And in our high-wrought modern narratives
> Stript of their harmonising soul, the life
> Of manners and familiar incidents,
> Had never much delighted me. And less
> Than other minds I had been used to owe
> The pleasure which I found in place or thing
> To extrinsic transitory accidents,
> Of record or tradition; but a sense
> Of what had been here done, and suffer'd here
> Through ages, and was doing, suffering, still
> Weigh'd with me, could support the test of thought,
> Was like the enduring majesty and power
> Of independent nature; and not seldom

Even indivual remembrances,
By working on the Shapes before my eyes
Became like vital functions of the soul;
And out of what had been, what was, the place
Was thronged with impregnations, like those wilds
In which my early feelings had been nurs'd,
And naked valleys, full of caverns, rocks,
And audible seclusions, dashing lakes,
Echoes and Waterfalls, and pointed crags
That into music touch the passing wind.
                    (*Prelude,* VIII, 769–95)

History is a presence whose weight is felt, but not understood in the immediacy of its revelation. Only later does the poet remember that this revelation was a 'thing divine'. His recollection of this event is the discovery of its significance. In the immediacy of revelation he is overwhelmed by the vast power of London's past, but in recollection he recovers that experience as the impregnation of an historical power present in the city as it lived for him in that moment.

Such a revelation of the city's past frees him from the immediate chaos of life there. It is a genuine liberation from everything trivial and vulgar. Most men living in the city are the victims and prisoners of the debased triviality of its life. But this is not the case for the man to whom it has been given to see the life there as only a part of a totality greater than itself. Such a vision preserves that man from becoming a slave to the immediate moment:

But though the picture weary out the eye,
By nature an unmanageable sight,
It is not wholly so to him who looks
In steadiness, who hath among least things
An under-sense of greatest; sees the parts
As parts, but with a feeling of the whole.
                    (*Prelude,* VII, 707–12)

This intuition of the 'whole' constitutes the freedom of the poet and of the man. Through it a significant world is recovered, a world invisible to the man caught up in the illusion which makes a part of life seem to be all of it. The revelation of the totality of things in the visitation of the imagination, and the discovery of the significance of that revelation in recollection liberate the poet from that illusion. The significant repetition of recollection frees him from the empty repetition of a life of 'endless imitation'. In this revelation the cacophony of the trivial intercourse of the city becomes a speech signifying 'higher things'.

Unknowingly the young Wordsworth crossed the threshold of London and encountered the massive weight of that city's historical presence. He was not aware of what had happened to him until it was over. The visitation of the imagination is not something that can be willed. It is always an unexpected usurpation succeeding a displacement in his perception of the world. Wordsworth and his companion were not aware that they had crossed the Alps either. In crossing the divide of the Alps Wordsworth encountered through the active intervention of the imagination the presence of 'infinitude' in the natural world:

> In such strength
> Of usurpation, in such visitings
> Of awful promise, when the light of sense
> Goes out in flashes that have shewn to us
> The invisible world, doth Greatness make abode,
> There harbours whether we be young or old.
> Our destiny, our nature, and our home
> Is with infinitude, and only there;
> *(Prelude,* VI, 532–39)

The invisible world revealed in the imagination's visitation is a universe of signs, an apocalyptic alphabet spelling out the relation of man's soul to the totality surrounding and sustaining it. The 'visible' world is the wild field where no indication of the divine can be read. In the revelations of the imagination the speech of the world is once more recovered:

> The immeasurable height
> Of woods decaying, never to be decay'd,
> The stationary blasts of water-falls,
> And every where along the hollow rent
> Winds thwarting winds, bewilder'd and forlorn,
> The torrents shooting from the clear blue sky,
> The rocks that mutter'd close upon our ears,
> Black drizzling crags that spake by the way-side
> As if a voice were in them, the sick sight
> And giddy prospect of the raving stream,
> The unfetter'd clouds, and region of the Heavens,

Tumult and peace, the darkness and the light
Were all like workings of one mind, the features
Of the same face, blossoms upon one tree,
Characters of the great Apocalypse,
The types and symbols of Eternity,
Of first and last, and midst, and without end.
                              (*Prelude*, VI, 556-72)

During the descent into Italy, after the visitation of the imagina-
tion, things in nature present themselves as 'if a voice were in
them'. What they are saying is that they are all parts of a single
totality, all elements in the 'workings of one mind'. The poet is
not always able to read or hear this language. For the most part it
belongs to a world closed off from him. The visitations of the
imagination are only intermittent, but they suffice. From them the
poet is able to intimate the presence of the world they indicate.
That world is there in the same way that the divide of the Alps was
there to be crossed, though the poet is not always aware of its
presence. The poet was not aware that he had crossed the Alps
until he had been so informed by the peasant he encountered. This
information compelled the discovery that he was displaced from
his customary relation to nature. It was not as it seemed to be.
This displacement becomes the scene where the visitation of the
imagination reveals the invisible presence of an infinite totality.
That presence is always there in nature, but it remains silent until
allowed to speak through the imagination. The world is divine,
but also hidden. One of those to whom it is revealed is the poet,
who is able to recover something of its speech in the language of
his poetry.

   As it was with his entrance into London, so it is only after the
crossing of the Alps, in remembering what had happened, that
Wordsworth is able to discover the 'glory' of what he saw. It is a
recognition in recollection that what was vouchsafed to him in
crossing the Simplon Pass was divine in origin. The presence of
the eternal in nature is felt at moments, points in time, and these
moments spread their influence over the course of the poet's life
like the rings formed by stones thrown one after the other into a
calmly flowing river. This intermittent, intervenient manifestation
of the eternal presence does not leave the poet with a clear sense of
the divine, but with a vague apprehension of something 'ever-
more about to be' (VI, 542). It is a life lived in the expectation of

the next visitation of the imagination which would grant to him once again a vision of the finite world as a part of a divine totality.

The visitation of the imagination is the repetition in the life of the man of the child's relation to the eternal. In the gaze of the child into infinity lies the figure of poetic inspiration for Wordsworth. For the child, unaware of death, there is no distinction between immortal and mortal, natural and divine. They are all one to him, to the point sometimes that the child cannot distinguish between the outer world and his own inner life. But the man possesses a consciousness of his own mortality, and it becomes the perspective which enables him to see the child's experience of the natural world as something divine. Death is the great division which enables the man to separate the mortal from the immortal. In recollection the child's immediate experience of the infinite is recovered with the accompanying awareness that the origin of that experience is divine.

In the 'Intimations Ode', as in *The Prelude*, there is a hidden world in which the finite, seemingly fragmentary, things of nature stand revealed in their relationship to a divine totality. But in the Ode this hidden world is not revealed through the visitations of the imagination. Nor is the revelation of that world contained within a dramatic moment as so often the visitations of the imagination are. The movement of the Ode, following the initial rush of the opening stanzas, is leisurely and meditative. This is clearly reflected in the way the poet moves back and forth among the manifold temporal dimensions of the poem. This movement does not lead up to any dramatic revelation. Its end is contained in its beginning; a question is asked and an answer is given. The answer is contained in the question in that the poet's discovery of his own mortality is the condition for discovering his immortality. This must be so, since the child remains oblivious to its mortality and unaware, consequently, that what it sees on first coming into the world is divine in origin. Only the man conscious of his mortality realizes the distinction between mortal and immortal life, between infinite and finite.

The Ode moves slowly and inevitably towards its end in the affirmation of the power of anamnesis to disclose in the child's early moments on earth the presence of the divine. In this affirmation of anamnesis' power lies the poet's redemption from the world into which he has fallen. The world the poet finds on stepping over the threshold of his childhood into a consciousness of his own mortality is a finite one articulated through an empty series of repetitive gestures. It is a diffuse world, and the things found within it seem to bear only an accidental relationship to one another. The presence of an ordering and uniting whole is not felt. A part of life is readily and easily confused for the whole of it.

In the 'intimations Ode' the poet affirms his discovery of the source, in recollection, of personal redemption from the conditions into which he fell upon realizing his own mortality. The basis for that affirmation is the disclosure in recollection of the meaning of his perception of the finite world as a child. The Ode has for its subject the fall and redemption of man told as a personal odyssey. This odyssey is the soul's search for the way back to its home after its discovery of its separation from God. At the heart of the Ode lies the mystery of how the One can become Many, how the soul awakens to find itself separated from the God who sent it into the world. Final separation from God is the impossible event, something that, given the nature of things, could not have happened. When it does happen it is regarded as an illusion, a temporary condition which can be rectified if one knows how to dispel the illusion, to penetrate the inner circles of the mystery surrounding the soul's loss of its divine origin. Wordsworth uses the figure of another mystery, birth and generation, to articulate the mystery of the soul's separation from God. It is through generation that the One of the philosophical tradition (in Plotinus' Third Ennead, for example) became the Many, that the god stepped off the mountain and became rain, that the Word was incarnate in Christ. In generation the eternal becomes temporal and finite, and the link between the natural and the divine is made manifest. But this link is also hidden and lost through the mystery of generation. Paradoxically, as the child grows toward heaven he relinquishes his intimate intercourse with the divine.

The poet, conscious of his own finitude, seeks to recover the lost threads of that intimate intercourse with the divine and cast off the burden of self-identity which becomes his in the realization of his separation from God. Self-identity has the heaviness of death about it. The conditions of life as they are realized in separation from God constitute an illusory denial of the fundamental unity of things in the One through whom they have their being. The realization of the soul's separation from God is followed by the discovery of the soul's primal affinity for God. In the poet's realization of his mortality lies the starting-point for his efforts to recover the primal intimacy between himself and God. He is nostalgic for what he has lost in becoming a man. This nostalgia determines the ways in which it is possible for him to regard his life on earth. In the 'Intimations Ode' there are two views of human life which present themselves successively to the poet's retrospective, nostalgic gaze. If the separation of the soul from God is absolute, then the world into which it has been sent is a prison-house, empty and meaningless. But if this separation is only an illusion, if the primal bond with God has never been broken, if the poet has only lost sight of it, then his life on earth becomes a journey through the world towards the eternal home of the soul. Yet before that journey can begin, the direction home must be found.

In the visible presence of the earth no directional markers are fixed. It is a place without identity from which every trace of the divine is absent. Through the power of anamnesis the poet discovers the hidden bond between the earth and the divine totality which sustains it:

> Those shadowy recollections,
>   Which, be they what they may,
> Are yet the fountain-light of all our day,
> Are yet a master-light of all our seeing;
>   Uphold us, cherish, and have power to make
> Our noisy years seem moments in the being
> Of the eternal Silence: truths that wake,
>   To perish never:
> Which neither listlessness, nor mad endeavour,
> Nor man nor Boy,
> Nor all that is at enmity with joy,
> Can utterly abolish or destroy!
>   Hence in a season of calm weather
>   Though inland far we be,
> Our Souls have sight of that immortal sea
>   Which brought us hither,
>   Can in a moment travel thither,
> And see the Children sport upon the shore,
> And hear the mighty waters rolling evermore.

What recollection recovers has the power to transform the poet's perception of his life on earth. He is liberated by it from the dreadful bonds of an empty and repetitious life. And though the child's vision is lost to the man, the significance of it is perpetually with him in recollection. The child possessed the vision of the eternal; the man inherits the meaning of it.

The poet has no clear knowledge of the nature of the totality revealed to him in recollection, only an intimation of its power and its eternity. This intimation is sufficient for him to achieve the 'philosophic mind' which, in the Socratic sense, has learned to die. Seen from the perspective determined by this intimation, death is no longer the absolute end of life, but a part of things through which the soul will travel, a stage upon its way back to its home. Wordsworth affirms this through the image of the 'Star' which in setting 'elsewhere', rises on earth with the birth of the child:

> Our birth is but a sleep and a forgetting:
> The Soul that rises with us, our life's Star,
>   Hath had elsewhere its setting,
>   And cometh from afar:

What remains unspoken is that when 'life's Star' sets on earth it will once again rise in the immortal skies of its eternal home. The soul is like a little immortal sun circling about its earth. Its rising and setting are the boundaries of its life on earth, but only moments in the course of its eternal life, where rising is setting, and setting, rising.

Wordsworth has not written a theological poem. The divine totality of which he speaks in the 'Intimations Ode', whose presence in recollection is powerful enough to alter the poet's view of life, remains ambiguous, something whose weight and pressure are felt but never clearly known. Heraclitus said of the Delphic oracle that it neither spoke out, nor concealed; but hinted. The totality of things revealed through the recollection of the child's perception of it is neither clearly disclosed nor finally concealed; it is intimated. Only its presence is affirmed by the poet, and its eternal nature. Beyond that he says nothing. The poet is granted an intuition into the hidden relationship of the finite to the infinite at that point where he stands utterly isolated, a single memory unto himself. His gaze is an inward one back into himself toward the point where recollection recovers those moments when a divine totality vouchsafed its presence to him. He is redeemed by that recollective gaze. His redemption remains uniquely his.

CHAPTER II

Wordsworth's Metaphors for Eternity: Appearance and Representation

What is it that tells my soul the Sun is setting?
'Prose Fragments', WORDSWORTH

Die Erscheinung ist das Entstehen und Vergehen, das
selbst nicht entsteht und vergeht, sondern an sich ist
und die Wirklichkeit und Bewegung des Lebens der
Wahrheit ausmacht. Das Wahre ist so der bacchan-
tische Taumel, an dem kein Glied nicht trunken ist;
und weil jedes, indem es sich absondert, ebenso unmit-
telbar (sich) auflöst, ist er ebenso die durchsichtige
und einfache Ruhe. In dem Gerichte jener Bewegung
bestehen zwar die einzelnen Gestalten des Geistes wie
die bestimmten Gedanken nicht, aber sie sind so sehr
auch positive notwendige Momente, als sie negativ
und verschwindend sind.—In dem *Ganzen* der Bewe-
gung, es als Ruhe aufgefasst, ist dasjenige, was sich
in ihr unterscheidet und besonderes Dasein gibt, als
ein solches, das sich *errinert*, aufbewahrt, dessen
Dasein das Wissen von sich selbst ist, wie dieses eb-
enso unmittelbar Dasein ist.

Phänomenologie des Geistes, HEGEL

[1]

THE nature and place of the activity of the imagination in Words-
worth's poetry have been at issue in several significant recent
interpretations of his work.[1] This chapter will attempt to articulate
clearly, through the act of the imagination represented in the

[1] Geoffrey H. Hartman, *Wordsworth's Poetry 1787–1814* (New Haven and London,
4th printing, 1971, with a new essay, 'Retrospect 1971'); Paul de Man, 'Wordsworth
und Hölderlin', *Schweizer Monatshefte*, 12 (1966), pp. 1141–55; J. Hillis Miller, 'The
Still Heart: Poetic Form in Wordsworth', *New Literary History*, 11 (1971), pp. 297–
310; Kenneth R. Johnston, 'The Idiom of Vision', in *New Perspectives on Coleridge and
Wordsworth*, ed. Geoffrey H. Hartman (New York and London, 1972).

'metaphor for eternity', one aspect of a large and difficult prob-
lem.[2] It presupposes temporarily one of the main theses of this
book: that the imagination is an act of mind constituted by the
mind's recollective recognition of its eternal nature. From this
recognition the power of the imagination arises. The metaphor
for eternity is the figural representation of that recognition.

In *The Prelude* Wordsworth speaks of a universe of analogies
which seems to be the matrix of a universal utterance linking
mind, nature, and the divine. Its ostensible ground is natural
analogy:

> A track pursuing not untrod before,
> From deep analogies by thought supplied,
> Or consciousness not to be subdued,
> To every natural form, rock, fruit or flower,
> Even the loose stones that cover the high-way,
> I gave a moral life, I saw them feel,
> Or link'd them to some feeling: the great mass
> Lay bedded in a quickening soul, and all
> That I beheld respired with inward meaning.
>
> . . . .
>
> . . . for I had an eye
> Which in my strongest workings, evermore
> Was looking for the shades of difference
> As they lie hid in all exterior forms,
> Near or remote, minute or vast, an eye
> Which from a stone, a tree, a wither'd leaf,
> To the broad ocean and the azure heavens,
> Spangled with kindred multitudes of stars,
> Could find no surface where its power might sleep,
> Which spake perpetual logic to my soul,
> And by an unrelenting agency,
> Did bind my feelings, even as in a chain.
>
> (*Prelude* III, 121–9; 156–67)

---

[2] My intention in this chapter is to explore the genesis of metaphor in Words-
worth's poetry of the imagination. The theoretical starting-point for it is Heidegger's
thinking through the transcendental scene of the open distance between intellect and
its object in the truth relationship, down to its unspoken sources in the *Wesen* and
Unwesen of truth, in his essay 'Vom Wesen der Wahrheit'. Two recent, very valuable
developments in the study of metaphor are situated within the Heideggerian prob-
lematic: Paul de Man's 'Genesis and Genealogy in Nietzsche's *The Birth of Tragedy*',
Diacritics, Winter, 1972; and Jacques Derrida's 'La Mythologie blanche', in the
collection of his essays entitled *Marges de la philosophie* (Paris, 1972).

'Exterior forms' conceal the ground of natural analogy; the action of eye and mind discloses it, and in this act the mind discovers the likeness of its own powers:

> I was a chosen Son.
> For hither I had come with holy powers
> And faculties, whether to work or feel:
> To apprehend all passions and all moods
> Which time, and place, and seasons do impress
> Upon the visible universe, and work
> Like changes there by force of my own mind.
> (*Prelude* III, 82–8)

The 'perpetual logic' of the eye retains nature as the ground of analogy generating the metaphor that articulates the hidden link of the mind to nature and the divine. The genesis of this image is represented as occurring within a natural teleology whose beginning and end is the eternal 'Presence' in nature. But the act of discovering analogies in the forms of visible nature reveals analogically the power of the mind to transform nature into an emblem of its own power; this power, whose meaning is disclosed in the mind's recollective recognition of it, becomes itself a sign of the divine origin and eternal nature of the soul.

Wordsworth calls these moments of revelation disclosing the connection of mind, nature, and the divine, the visitations of the imagination. In them the imagination, not nature, becomes the ground of analogy. Images are transposed upon the 'celestial soil' of the imagination. The metaphor for eternity is not generated from analogies between images in the natural field: nature, and its inherent teleology, is abandoned for the syntax of the appearances of things as they seem to the eye of the imagination. The syntax of imaginative appearances supplants the 'perpetual logic' of a universe of natural utterance; a natural system of associations, with their implicit teleology aiming at the divine, is the ostensible mode in which the mind represents the creative activity of the imagination to itself, but this mode is perpetually subverted by a logic of things as they appear to the eye of the imagination.

Of all Wordsworth's metaphors, the ones through which the image of eternity is generated are the most precarious. They no longer depend upon the solid ground of natural representation and the processes of analogy found in nature, but rise freely out of

the unstable and infrequent occasion of an 'unconscious inter-
course' with the divine manifested in the visitation of the imagi-
nation and articulated through the presence of the accidental
appearances of natural things. In the play of light upon water, in
the magnifications of mountain mists, and in the radiance of set-
ting suns he found a language valid for eternity, whose source of
significance, in the visitations of the imagination, remained largely
unconscious and unspoken, except when disclosed to conscious-
ness through specific acts of recollection. The 'divine analogy'[3]
which Wordsworth's Eighteenth-Century predecessors read off
from the laws governing the essential motions and aspects of
nature (i.e. that God's love for man was as constant as the attrac-
tion of the earth's gravity, etc.), was for him mute and blank.
Wordsworth's imagination was not dependent upon or sub-
servient to what was conceived as essential in nature, but freely
took advantage of the appearances of things manifested through
the play of accidental conjunctions in the natural field. By con-
fiscating these appearances, the imagination becomes the 'celestial'
ground from which spring those metaphors in the 'Poems of the
Imagination' able to generate a sense of the divine and the infinite.

The way in which the metaphor for eternity generates a sense of
the divine and infinite can be elaborated through Wordsworth's
metaphor of the soul as the star of life in the 'Intimations Ode':

> Our birth is but a sleep and a forgetting:
> The Soul that rises with us, our life's Star,
> > Hath had elsewhere its setting,
> > And cometh from afar:
> > Not in entire forgetfulness,
> > And not in utter nakedness,
> But trailing clouds of glory do we come
> > From God, who is our home:
> Heaven lies about us in our infancy!
> Shades of the prison-house begin to close
> > Upon the growing Boy,
> But He beholds the light, and whence it flows,
> > He sees it in his joy;
> The Youth, who daily farther from the east
> > Must travel, still is Nature's Priest,

3 Cf. Earl R. Wasserman's 'Nature Moralized: The Divine Analogy in the Eighteenth Century', *ELH*, vol. xx, No. 1, 1953, pp. 39–76.

And by the vision splendid
Is on his way attended;
At length the Man perceives it die away,
And fade into the light of common day.
                              (V, 58–76)

The metaphor of the soul as 'life's Star' is constituted through a complex and ambiguous interplay of images generated by the way in which the light of the rising star differs in appearance from that of the star when it has progressed some distance along its orbit. It is the difference between the light of the rising sun transfiguring the earth, making it a field of light from which spring those 'first-born' affinities between the mind and its new world, and the light of the sun overhead illuminating the earth with the 'light of common day'. The metaphor of the soul/star, formed from the difference between two appearances of the same thing, dominates the movement of the whole poem. It is the figure which transforms the linearity of mortality into the circularity of eternal life. The metonymic perception of a fragmented and disjointed world reappears 'circumfused' within a metaphoric vision of eternity.

The soul/star is a metaphor generating the image of a totality, of the continuity of the mortal and the immortal. Rising, the soul/star is the point of mediation between heaven and earth, life and death, finite and infinite. Though its light is insufficient and dies out and is commuted into the light of common day, it lives on yet in memory, the remembered radiance of sunrise in the stark light of noon. Life, the journey of the soul, is a sleep and a forgetting; it is the journey of the sun through the land of the dead. What keeps the poet alive in this dark world of the grave is the act of recollection which preserves the image of the soul's original light. He has a quasi-Gnostic fear, almost, that if the light were not somehow preserved in recollection, escape from the alien world through which his soul travels would not be possible.

The youth is the fire carrier, 'Nature's Priest', and is the link between the divine and nature; yet he unites the two in a curiously ambiguous fashion. The youth perceives a glory in nature; it is the scene where the radiant beauty and sublime terror of the divine shimmer in a field of light stretching before him. Yet nature is hostile and inimical in its beneficence towards the youth; its only aim is to make him forget whence he has come and take what comfort he can in its barren presence. He is like a guilty thing facing that accommodating solicitude, alien and unable to perceive in nature the end and purpose of his being, ever on the verge of going beyond it. The natural world manifests the absence of the divine, and yet that absence, felt along the senses as the absence of nature's former radiance, is the perpetual reminder of the divine. The natural world is the way away from God as the youth steps westward toward death, but it is also the way to God. It is the starting-point for recollection's backward glance, which frees the man from the natural perspective and places him within the eternal silence, the perfect orbit of his immortal liberty.

This journey, then, from east to west, from immortal life to immortal life, is grasped as the passage of a sun across the heavens. The rising and setting of the sun are seen only as moments in the eternal course of things, parts marked out in an infinite orbit, but yet never really separated from it. The orbit of the sun is linked, in Wordsworth's metaphor, to the soul's trajectory as it passes through the natural world. The sun in its orbit, a natural image, articulates the course of the soul, but nature itself, as we have seen, manifests both the absence and, as reminder, the trace of the divine. In themselves, natural images seem to be empty. It is the act of the imagination which transforms them into the types and representatives of eternity. The power of the star/soul metaphor to generate a sense of eternity is not derived immediately from the natural image of the sun, but mediately from what is revealed in nature through the activity of the imagination and its subsequent interpretation in the act of recollection.

[11]

A natural image is taken up into the imagination's sphere in the same way that the soul makes its entrance into the body, as a seed planted in an alien soil. The soul, Wordsworth tells us (*Prelude*, III, 181), is a seed planted in an alien ground where it must send forth those shoots and tendrils which will form the bond between itself and the 'wild field' into which it has fallen. This is one metaphor which controls Wordsworth's perception of the soul's relation to nature. The image of infinity is not generated from nature, but from the advent of infinity into nature. It is a paracletic visitation. In the 'Preface to the Edition of 1815' Wordsworth says that the imagination, with its power to modify, create, and associate, becomes the celestial soil in which images, arising from the co-operative interaction of internal feeling and external accident, are planted, 'commutated', and transferred for immortality:

> . . . in the series of Poems placed under the head of Imagination, I have begun with one of the earliest processes of Nature in the development of this faculty. Guided by one of my own primary consciousnesses, I have represented a commutation and transfer of internal feelings, co-operating with external accidents, to plant, for immortality, images of sound and sight, in the celestial soil of the Imagination. The Boy, there introduced, is listening, with something of a feverish and restless anxiety, for the recurrence of the riotous sounds which he had previously excited; and, at the moment when the intenseness of his mind is beginning to remit, he is surprised into a perception of the solemn and tranquilizing images which the Poem describes. [*The reference here is to the poem*, 'There was a Boy'.][4]

The soul, once itself a seed, has become through the active power of the imagination a celestial field in which natural images are planted. Seed is planted within seed, and the seed itself becomes a ground. The earth, once the field, is now the seed, and the soul, once a seed, is a field. One metaphor grows from the other, and it is the metaphor of growth, in both instances, which forms the link between the celestial and the terrestrial. The genetic metaphor constitutes the link between the soul and nature, yet it is also the ground from out of which arises the power of the soul to go beyond nature. This metamorphic drift, freed as it were from the representation of real organic growth and generation, where seed becomes ground, and ground, seed, does not move within the natural sphere, but between it and the source disclosing the totality of things through imaginative revelation. Imagination, we shall see, is the seedbed of metaphor, but the imaginative act creating metaphor from natural images is also the act which transcends the natural. The metaphor which generates the image of eternity is not dependent upon any essential aspect of nature, but seizes upon its accidental aspects.

Wordsworth's discussion of the powers of the imagination in the 'Preface of 1815' falls into two parts. The first is a description

---

[4] 'Preface to the Edition of 1815', in *The Prose Works of William Wordsworth*, ed. W. J. B. Owen and Jane Worthington Smyser (Oxford, 1974), vol. III, p. 35. Hereafter *The Prose Works* will be cited as *Pr.W.*

of the 'conferring, the abstracting and the modifying powers of the Imagination, immediately and mediately acting'[5] upon images independent of one another, and then in conjunction with each other. Its sphere is restricted to the analogical, to identities discoverable as inherent in natural objects and elicited through the power of the imagination to discover and unify them. The second part concerns what he calls the 'full strength of the imagination'[6] operating in the image of Satan flying, which Wordsworth takes from Book II of *Paradise Lost:*

> As when far off at sea a fleet descried
> *Hangs* in the clouds, by equinoctial winds
> Close sailing from Bengala, or the isles
> Of Ternate or Tidore, whence merchants bring
> Their spicy drugs; they on the trading flood
> Through the wide Ethiopian to the Cape
> Ply, stemming nightly toward the Pole: so seemed
> Far off the flying Fiend.

Wordsworth's commentary upon these lines is as follows:

Here is the full stength of the imagination involved in the word *hangs*, and exerted upon the whole image: First, the fleet, an aggregate of many ships, is represented as one mighty person, whose track, we know and feel, is upon the waters; but, taking advantage of its appearance to the senses, the poet dares to represent it as *hanging in the clouds,* both for the gratification of the mind in contemplating the image itself, and in reference to the motion and appearance of the sublime object to which it is compared.[7]

The imagination has become creative; no longer does it represent nature by imitating it. It separates itself from a dependence upon natural objects and their inherent qualities, and *takes advantage* of their appearance to the senses to render commensurately the 'motion and appearance' of a sublime object. How, Wordsworth asks later in the same essay, does the imagination shape and create in this fashion? His answer is:

By innumerable processes; and in none does it more delight than in that of consolidating numbers into unity, and dissolving and separating unity into number,—alternations proceeding from, and governed by, a

[5] Ibid., p. 33.
[6] Ibid., p. 31.
[7] Ibid.

sublime consciousness of the soul in her own mighty and almost divine powers. Recur to the passage already cited from Milton. When the compact Fleet, as one Person, has been introduced 'Sailing from Bengala,' 'They,' *i.e.* the 'merchants,' representing the fleet resolved into a multitude of ships, 'ply' their voyage towards the extremities of the earth: 'So,' (referring to the word 'As' in the commencement) 'seemed the flying Fiend;' the image of his Person acting to recombine the multitude of ships into one body,—the point from which the comparison set out. 'So seemed,' and to whom seemed? To the heavenly Muse who dictates the poem, to the eye of the Poet's mind, and to that of the Reader, present at one moment in the wide Ethiopian, and the next in the solitudes, then first broken in upon, of the infernal regions!
'Modo me Thebis, modo ponit Athenis.'[8]

The esemplastic power of the imagination is linked once again with the appearances of natural objects ('So seemed') and not with the real qualities inhering in them. This power to create a unified totality to which the elements of a poem belong, both retaining their integral individuality and yet participating in the whole which sustains them, is the one which Coleridge identifies as the dominant activity of the primary imagination in the *Biographia Literaria*. Wordsworth identifies it with the capacity of the poet to take advantage of the appearances of things.[9] In the 'Essay, Supplementary to the Preface' he is even more explicit:

The appropriate business of poetry, (which, nevertheless, if genuine, is as permanent as pure science,) her appropriate employment, her privilege and her *duty*, is to treat of things not as they *are*, but as they *appear*; not as they exist in themselves, but as they *seem* to exist to the *senses*, and to the *passions*. What a world of delusion does this acknowledged obligation prepare for the inexperienced! . . .[10]

In the 'Preface of 1815' Wordsworth rejected the conception of the imagination, which Taylor gave in his *British Synonyms discriminated*, as a simple imaging faculty capable only of distinctly copying sense impressions. To conceive of it this way is, Wordsworth felt, to make it a mere mode of memory. Imagination is, in

[8] Ibid., pp. 33–4.

[9] Cf. '. . . the pleasure which the mind derives from the perception of similitude in dissimilitude. This principle is the great spring of the activity of our minds and their chief feeder.' 'Preface to Lyrical Ballads (1800)', in *Pr.W.*, vol. i, p. 148.

[10] Ibid., vol. iii, p. 63.

essence, the act which frees man from a dependence upon particular natural figures and their qualities, and allows him to transcend them toward the infinite (the sublime) by taking advantage of their appearances.

Imagination is that awareness of totality (the One in the Many) and relationship which frees the poet from fancy, from a slavery to the imitation of the images of the natural world as they are in themselves, and gives to him the liberty to generate metaphorically through their appeances the types and representatives of immortality. This going beyond things themselves to their appearances is a form of transcendence whose ground is the imagination's celestial soil.

[III]

Nature is not the cause, but the occasion for poetry. The imagination seizes upon the accidental conjunctions of things in nature, takes them up, and subsumes them under the higher laws of its operation. Natural images, and even the human figure apprehended in certain attitudes, are converted, or commuted, by the act of the imagination into an apocalyptic alphabet, in which, in silence, is read the presence of the holy. The gravitation of Wordsworth's imagination toward the permanent and enduring forms of nature,[11] and of personal and national history, as images of the eternal, in its relation to the sublime, is the more traditional aspect of his poetic practice. Not only the image of 'woods decaying, never to be decayed', but the figure of 'native Man', the shepherd, in the presence of nature and of God, becomes the image of the eternal:

> Seeking the raven's nest, and suddenly
> Surpris'd with vapours, or on rainy days
> When I have angled up the lonely brooks
> Mine eyes have glanced upon him, few steps off,
> In size a giant, stalking through the fog,
> His Sheep like Greenland Bears; at other times
> When round some shady promontory turning,
> His Form hath flash'd upon me, glorified

[11] Josephine Miles has made a very perceptive study of this aspect of Wordsworth's imagery in her *Wordsworth and the Vocabulary of Emotion*, University of California Publications in English, vol. XII, pp. 43–52.

> By the deep radiance of the setting sun:
> Or him have I descried in distant sky,
> A solitary object and sublime,
> Above all height! like an aerial Cross,
> As it is stationed on some spiry Rock
> Of the Chartreuse, for worship.
>
> (*Prelude*, VIII, 396–409)

Yet these images of man and natural things are not in themselves permanent, but only seem so. They are things which the poet happens upon by accident, which take him by surprise, and whose appearance in those moments he is able to convert into the language of eternity.[12] The shepherd is transfigured by the setting sun, and his sheep are magnified by the fog. The sun will set, and the fog will burn off, yet the images manifesting the divine will remain behind, responsive to the significances which recollection will disclose in them.

In his essay on Victor Hugo in *Réflexions sur quelques-uns des mes contemporains*, Baudelaire speculates about the nature of what he calls 'les mystères de l'*analogie*'. In a series of reflective leaps, from Fourier to Swedenborg to Lavater, he arrives at the truth (*cette vérité*) that, 'tout est hiéroglyphique, et nous savons que les symboles ne sont obscurs que d'une manière relative, c'est-à-dire selon la pureté, la bonne volonté ou la clairvoyance native des âmes.'[13] The poet is the translator and decipherer of the hieroglyphics which constitute the universe. Everything is translatable into something or even ultimately everything else.

---

[12] Cf. this passage on Furness Abbey and its natural setting: 'So that in this respect the images of Nature would unite with the cloistral architecture to shut up the Soul within itself & to assist the Devotee in the task of mortification & the relinquishment of worldly pleasures; and in contrast to this seclusion, if a magnificent prospect of Mountains & the plain of the Ocean may be supposed—in spite of an oppressive routine of rites & ceremonies—not to have been lost upon the mind, but to have contributed to the devotional feeling by a display of the sublimest work of the Creator & by holding forth shadows & sensible types or representations of that infinity which is the true element & birthright of the human soul, an opportune station for participating this advantage was not wanting. . . . Or if the habitual listlessness & indolence of the cloister accompanied the solitary visitant to this eminence, though too passive to seek for amusement in the creations of his own thoughts, he might still not be insensible to the Changes in the appearances of things which Nature would be carrying forward before his eyes. A gleam of light striking upon the distant Towers of Lancaster, . . .' in 'An Unpublished Tour', *Pr.W.*, vol. II, pp. 296–7.

[13] 'Réflexions sur quelques-uns de mes contemporains', *Œuvres complètes de Baudelaire*, ed. Y.-G. Le Dantec and Claude Pichois (Paris, 1961), p. 705.

Chez les excellents poëtes, il n'y a pas de métaphore, de comparaison ou d'épithète qui ne soit d'une adaptation mathématiquement exacte dans la circonstance actuelle, parce que ces comparaisons, ces métaphores et ces épithètes sont puisées dans l'inépuisable fonds de l'*universelle analogie*, et qu'elles ne peuvent être puisées ailleurs.[14]

For Baudelaire the space of transcendence, the distance between the poet and his universe, is bridged in the act of decipherment. The universe of hieroglyphs reposes upon the inexhaustible ground of an identity immanent and coextensive with everything that is. The poet is the privileged interpreter of that world, whose obscurity is only relative to the capacity of the individual soul to penetrate it. Given a soul of ample magnitude, everything would be transparently identical with everything else. It is a possibility latent within the world in which the poet finds himself, and is not dependent upon him for its meaning, but only for its translation, which is only a version of its meaning.

For Wordsworth, in contradistinction, nature remains an ambiguous term. In itself nature is silent, and the divine is absent from it. Yet nature becomes for the poet a language in which the divine may be read. What is revealed through the mediation of nature is the divine, but what nature is in itself is elided. Nature is inscribed with a holy script, not through what is essential to it, but by its accidental appearances. The meaning of that language is not immanent in nature, but becomes visible only when transplanted on to the soil of the imagination. Nature is commuted by the action of the imagination, functioning at its fullest power, into that 'great Nature' which is to be found in the work of 'mighty poets'. Restricted to the sphere of nature, the imagination forms metaphors which remain within the range of natural analogy, however greatly extended or complex that might become. But when the power of the imagination is fully present, the ground of the analogy between the divine and the natural is obliterated and the freely creative imagination subsumes the appearances of nature under the workings of its visionary power. From these appearances the metaphor of eternity is generated and the link between the finite and the infinite is made manifest.

Nature becomes the image of the divine when it ceases to be nature, and comes to reside only in its accidental appearances.

[14] Ibid.

Nature is a single term, and the image in nature retains its individual integrity; but when the image is taken by the imagination its presence as a thing in nature is supressed. In the eye of the imagination exercising its fullest powers, the two natures (as it is in itself and as it appears through accidental conjunctions) cannot coexist. One is passed over by the other and forgotten. Nature taken in itself is supplanted by its own appearances. The difference between the two natures, between essence and accident, is taken by the imagination as a manifestation of the divine.

Two images, one from Wordsworth's prose and the other taken from his poetry, will, I think, make this process of commutation more explicit. The first is the image of the rock in the Rhine at the fall of Chafhausen found in a prose fragment on the sublime and the beautiful which forms a part of 'An Unpublished Tour'. The second is the recurrent image of nature as a book in Wordsworth's poetry.

The sublime, Wordsworth asserts in a fragment on the sublime and beautiful, is a sensation which can be analysed into three component and interdependent parts:

... a sense of individual form or forms; a sense of duration; and a sense of power. The whole complex impression is made up of these elementary parts, & the effect depends upon their co-existence. For, if any one of them were abstracted, the others would be deprived of their power to affect.[15]

When analysed, the sensation of the sublime is complex, but the experience of it is simple. The consummation of the experience of the sublime is an intense feeling of unity in which the separations among the elements of the sublime are dissolved: 'For whatever suspends the comparing power of the mind & possesses it with a feeling or image of intense unity, without a conscious contemplation of parts, has produced that state of mind which is the consummation of the sublime'.[16]

Infinity, Wordsworth goes on to say, is a modification of unity. It is the sense of power which effects this modification. Power is of two kinds: that which is to be resisted morally, and actively, and consequently regarded as that which will eventually be rendered evanescent in an absolute triumph over it; and that

15 *Pr.W.*, vol. II, p. 351.
16 Ibid., pp. 353–4.

power, experienced passively, in which participation is imaginatively possible. It is the latter form of the sublime sensation of power which interests Wordsworth, for in it he has discovered a form of manifest approximation to absolute unity. This mode of the sublime resides for him in the resistance to the waters of the Rhine by the rock in the middle of the fall at Chafhausen. All of the elements of the sublime—duration, individual form, and a sense of power—coexist in that image of the rock and the fall, which undergoes a modification toward infinity when seen through the eye of the imagination:

If the resistance contemplated be of a passive nature (such, for example, as the Rock in the middle of the fall of the Rhine at Chafhausen, as opposed for countless ages to that mighty mass of Waters), there are undoubtedly here before us two distinct images & thoughts; & there is a most complex instrumentality acting upon the senses, such as the roar of the Water, the fury of the foam, &c.; and an instrumentality still more comprehensive, furnished by the imagination, & drawn from the length of the River's course, the Mountains from which it rises, the various countries thro' which it flows, & the distant Seas in which its waters are lost. These images & thoughts will, in such a place, be present to the mind, either personally or by representative abstractions more or less vivid.—Yet to return to the rock & the Waterfall: these objects will be found to have exalted the mind to the highest state of sublimity when they are thought of in that state of opposition & yet reconcilement, analogous to parallel lines in mathematics, which, being infinitely prolonged, can never come nearer to each other; & hence, tho' the images & feelings above enumerated have exerted a preparative influence upon the mind, the absolute crown of the impression is infinity, which is a modification of unity.[17]

What begins in a very particular act of attentive perception focusing on the flow of the water and the presence of the rock in its midst is transformed by the eye of the imagination into the *force* of the water and the *resistance* of the rock. Imaginative participation generates a moral modification of a natural scene. The temporal endurance of the rock and the spatial extension of the waters playing about it form two parallel lines leading off toward infinity. It is the power of the waters, imaginatively extended, which endows the resistance of the rock with anything like a

[17] Ibid., pp. 356–7.

permanent endurance. The rock is embedded in the river the way
a natural image is planted in the soil of the imagination. What
emerges is the manifest approximation to unity, the intimation,
that is, through the action of the imagination upon the appear-
ances of nature, of infinitude at the point where the parallel lines
of force and resistance meet in the sensation of infinity. They
become the emblem of the mind's power and infinitude. Infinity
is not to be found in nature, but intimated from the way the eye
of the imagination interprets what it discovers. Imaginative per-
ception happens in the coincidence of an internal state and an
external occurrence. In this coincidence the time and space belong-
ing to natural objects and the perception of them are commuted
into a mathematical space whose emblem is two parallel lines. The
finite is transformed into an approximation of the infinite through
the imaginative interpretation of its active presence.

The imaginative commutation of the rock and the fall at
Chafhausen subsumes under a moral purpose the perception of a
natural process.[18] The rock, ceasing to be a rock, becomes resis-
tance to the power of the Rhine, which ceases to be a natural
phenomenon, and becomes the force of waters stretching in
imagination from their source remote in the Alps to their debou-
chure in the distant and somewhat abstract seas. River and rock
become parallel emblems of the infinite, tandem auxiliars of the
divine. This form of imaginative commutation begins in a close
perception of a very complex sensation, and leads away from it,
through the attribution of moral qualities to natural events (by

---

[18] Cf. this quasi-Platonic passage from *The Excursion,* Book IV:

> For, the Man—
> Who, in this spirit, communes with the Forms
> Of nature, who with understanding heart
> Both knows and loves such objects as excite
> No morbid passions, no disquietude,
> No vengeance, and no hatred—needs must feel
> The joy of that pure principle of love
> So deeply, . . .   (1207–14)
>
> .   .   .   .
>
>   The light of love
> Not failing, perseverance from their steps
> Departing not, for them shall be confirmed
> The glorious habit by which sense is made
> Subservient still to moral purposes,
> Auxiliar to divine.
>   (1244–49)

which event becomes act), toward the simple and unified. The modifying and conferring powers of the imagination transform and unify what is seen in nature. Yet it is clear that the full strength of the imagination is not present and active in the description of the fall at Chafhausen, for if it were it would have affected the poet's immediate perception of things in nature and would not have begun from a complex perception which could then be subsequently modified.

In the moments after the visitation of the imagination, when the poet is still possessed by the full power of revelation, nature appears to him as a holy writing, an apocalyptic alphabet, from which the divine and immortal may be read. The best known of such moments in Wordsworth's work is the descent from the divide of the Alps through the Simplon Pass in Book VI of *The Prelude*. Wordsworth employs the very ancient topos of the book of nature, whose ultimate authority in the Western tradition is St. Paul's Letter to the Romans, to articulate the idiosyncratic form of his vision. In Book I of *The Excursion* there is a moment which is in many respects structurally and ontologically identical to the descent from the Alps; in it possession by the living God is followed by a vision of nature as a form of holy writing:

> —Far and wide the clouds were touched,
> And in their silent faces could he read
> Unutterable love. Sound needed none,
> Nor any voice of joy; his spirit drank
> The spectacle: sensation, soul, and form,
> All melted into him; they swallowed up
> His animal being; in them did he live,
> And by them did he live; they were his life.
> In such access of mind, in such high hour
> Of visitation from the living God,
> Thought was not; in enjoyment it expired.
> No thanks he breathed, he proffered no request;
> Rapt into still communion that transcends
> The imperfect offices of prayer and praise,
> His mind was a thanksgiving to the power
> That made him; it was blessedness and love!
>   A Herdsman on the lonely mountaintops,
> Such intercourse was his, and in this sort
> Was his existence oftentimes *possessed*.

O then how beautiful, how bright, appeared
The written promise! Early had he learned
To reverence the volume that displays
The mystery, the life which cannot die;
But in the mountains did he *feel* his faith.
All things, responsive to the writing, there
Breathed immortality, revolving life,
And greatness still revolving; infinite:
There littleness was not; the least of thing;
Seemed infinite; and there his spirit shaped
Her prospects, nor did he believe,—he *saw*.

(*The Excursion*, I, 203–32)

This is the vision of a 'natural poet', one endowed with the powers of the imagination, but lacking the accomplishment of verse.[19] What the herdsman reads in nature, in effect, supplants what he has read in the Bible. What he reads in nature is the inscription of the immediate presence of the holy; what he read in the Bible was mediated through faith. Believing is not seeing, but seeing is something more than believing. The book of nature is commensurate with his soul's immensity, with the visionary faculty he possesses or is possessed by, while the language of the holy scripture stands between him and the presence of God. The written language of men is seen as a diminution of the holy, inadequate to its representation. In the act of reading the presence of the holy in nature, the consummation of the marriage of mind and nature (foretold in the preface to *The Excursion*) is enacted; yet it is not nature in itself that is read, but nature transfigured by the revelation of the imagination, the visitation of God. The image of man and nature is, Wordsworth tells us, poetry, and, he could add, the reading of the holy in nature is a living poetry more enduring than the poetry found in the books of man.

Book V of *The Prelude*, 'Books', begins with a curious fancy of very serious import for Wordsworth:

Hitherto,
In progress through this Verse, my mind hath look'd
Upon the speaking face of earth and heaven
As her prime Teacher, intercourse with man
Establish'd by the sovereign Intellect,
Who through that bodily Image hath diffus'd

---

[19] *The Excursion*, I, 76–80.

A soul divine which we participate,
A deathless spirit. Thou also, Man, hast wrought,
For commerce of thy nature with itself,
Things worthy of unconquerable life;
And yet we feel, we cannot chuse but feel
That these must perish.   (10–21)
. . . .
                    Oh! why hath not the mind
Some element to stamp her image on
In nature somewhat nearer to her own?
Why, gifted with such powers to send abroad
Her spirit, must it lodge in shrine so frail?
                                        (44–8)

The language of the poet, housed in fragile and vulnerable books, is inferior to the 'speaking face' of nature. The speech of men, speaking to themselves, is incommensurate with the everlasting depth and reach of their inner being. In nature, seen as an inscribed language, there is a speech more equal to the immortal presence of man's soul. But it is a speech he cannot manipulate, and he must therefore employ a lesser language for an archetype of nature.[20] The language of the poet is a clearly diminished speech, and stands between the poet and a more direct expression of the divine and holy revealed to him through the imagination's visitations. The poet can, in the end, only 'make breathings' for what lies within and without him. In fantasy he would like to transform the face of nature into a blank book into which he could inscribe the visionary; but how and with what instrument would he impress upon nature his visionary poetry? Wordsworth does not know. He knows only that nature, in certain privileged moments is a superior form of writing, and is seen as such through imaginative revelation.

In these moments of imaginative revelation, when nature becomes a holy book, what nature is in itself is elided in order that the divine inscription might become visible. In nature, and in the vision of man in nature, this language becomes visible in a movement away from the particular and multiple, toward individual

[20] Cf. 'Essays upon Epitaphs', II, p. 77, and III, pp. 84–5, *Pr.W.*, vol. II. Here, adumbrated, is a view of language as the incarnation of thought, which in turn is an archetype (or mirror image, as the image of a tree reflected from the surface of a lake is its archetype) of what is perceived. Language is thus removed from the natural sphere, and has dominion only over its images and reflections.

(self-begetting) and singular figures. The mind is led away from
the confusing multeity of particular things without relation to one
another, toward the great simple forms of nature which embody
relationship and indicate the totality of things to which they
belong: rivers, lakes, clouds, mountains, moonlight, and sun-
light. This movement of the mind constitutes a separation of what
is permanent and great in man and nature, from what is ephemeral
and trivial. In an earlier version of the preface to *The Excursion*
Wordsworth invokes the Soul of man to teach him to, 'discern
and part/Inherent things from casual, what is fixed/From fleeting,
that my verse may live . . .'[21] This discernment is essential to the
formation of the poetry of the imagination.

The human figure in the presence of nature, natural man, stands
singular, lordly, and isolate. Like the shepherd, he stands free
from the encumbering triviality of social life, from its passing
fashions and mobile manners, from its essential transitoriness.
Such a singular and isolate figure, stripped of everything in-
essential, seen standing high up on a mountainside, in a fog, or
silhouetted against the radiance of the setting sun, is a seed, an
external and accidental appearance, ready to be planted in the soil
of the imagination and commuted by that implantation into the
type and representation of immortality. No longer 'native Man'
in the presence of nature, he is a holy image transfigured upon the
mountain.

[IV]

There is, I think, one other aspect of the metaphor for eternity in
Wordsworth's poetry which it is necessary for us to look at: the
image of light. We began with the 'life's Star' of the 'Intimations
Ode', and perhaps by ending with it we shall come full circle,
however elliptically it may be drawn. The soul in the 'Intimations
Ode' is a star, a sun, which, in setting in the skies of eternity, rises
upon earth and begins its procession toward immortality. Preces-
sion becomes, as it were, procession. This metaphor for the soul's
immortal life is based upon the appearance of a natural object and
not upon the nature of the thing itself. The appearance of the sun
over the eastern horizon and its westward-stepping disappearance
beyond the western presupposes here a geocentric orbit. When the

sun disappears, however, in a geocentric movement, the customary supposition is that it continues in its orbit about, or under, the earth; yet the orbit of Wordsworth's star, swinging between the infinite and the finite, is more like the elliptical orbit of a comet racing suddenly into the gravitational field of the sun, where it first becomes visible, remaining there for a time, and then departing as quickly as it came.

Wordsworth takes imaginative advantage of the aura of the unknown which is a part of the sensation surrounding the sun's disappearance. In setting the sun moves, if only in terms of sensation and feeling, beyond the edge of the known into the unknown. The appearance of its disappearance is what Wordsworth uses to generate the sense of a link between the finite and the infinite. The progression toward the unknown present in the light of the setting sun forms the imaginative link between heaven and earth. The soul has its orbit, as has the sun, and as the sun, in setting, disappears into the unknown, so will the soul. That disappearance, as appearance, becomes a metaphorical springboard into eternity.

The sun's orbit, and its departing light, become a part of the play of appearances in the 'Intimations Ode' through which the imagination generates the image of eternity. The shimmer and dance of light upon natural things and the imagination's response to it, as though like were answering the muted call to like, form an experience whose constancy and obscure significance make it one of the decisive events of Wordsworth's creative activity. In the accidental flash of light transfiguring the face of nature Wordsworth found a manifest (if approximate) link between the soul and the external universe, and beyond that, a bond between the natural world and the divine. The identity of the soul with its immortal origin shines in the light which penetrates and transforms its reflectors. God is present in the light of setting suns, and in the shimmering moonlight upon the sands of Westmoreland where the young Wordsworth stood as a stranger in a field of light holding unconscious intercourse with it.[22]

There are two passages, one in 'Home at Grasmere', and the other in the first book of *The Excursion*, written within a period of approximately two years (1797–98/1800), where the natural world becomes a field of light and the link between the soul and nature,

[22] *The Prelude*, I, 594–608.

and between the natural and the divine is made manifest. In the
first (and later) passage the line separating image from reality is
lost, and the natural scene becomes the sheer image of its light-
engendered appearances:

> —How vast the compass of this theatre,
> Yet nothing to be seen but lovely pomp
> And silent majesty; the birch-tree woods
> Are hung with thousand thousand diamond drops
> Of melted hoar-frost, every tiny knot
> In the bare twigs, each little budding-place
> Cased with its several bead, what myriads there
> Upon one tree, while all the distant grove
> That rises to the summit of the steep
> Shows like a mountain built of silver light.
> See yonder the same pageant, and again
> Behold the universal imagery
> Inverted, all its sun-bright features touched
> As with the varnish, and the gloss of dreams;
> Dreamlike the blending also of the whole
> Harmonious landscape; all along the shore
> The boundary lost, the line invisible
> That parts the image from reality;
> And the clear hills, as high as they ascend
> Heavenward, so piercing deep the lake below.
>   ('Home at Grasmere', 560–79)[23]

The compass of this scene is indeed vast, and the dream is of
infinity. The birch-tree woods become a 'mountain built of silver
light' whose image, rising toward the heavens, is inverted by the
lake beneath it, which reflects the image of that image. This
natural theatre has become a spectacle of images, and the poet is
spectator and participant in their 'bacchanalia'; his imagination
becomes the dancing ground of that dreamlike play. It is a game
played in the field of appearances, where image gives birth to
image, as seed generates seed, in a figural dance of the imagination.
But it is a game from which the natural world has been essentially
excluded. As the ground of analogy nature is the pretext for it,
but it is quickly left behind.

In Book I of *The Excursion* there is a similar moment where the
earth and the heavens become a single image in a liquid bath of

light. This moment belongs to a stage in the growth of the natural poet, and is represented as a 'visitation from the living God'.[24]

> Such was the Boy—but for the growing Youth
> What soul was his, when, from the naked top
> Of some bold headland, he beheld the sun
> Rise up, and bathe the world in light! He looked—
> Ocean and earth, the solid frame of earth
> And ocean's liquid mass, in gladness lay
> Beneath him:—Far and wide the clouds were touched,
> And in their silent faces could he read
> Unutterable love. Sound needed none,
> Nor any voice of joy; his spirit drank
> The spectacle: sensation, soul, and form,
> All melted into him; they swallowed up
> His animal being; in them did he live,
> And by them did he live; they were his life.
>
> (*The Excursion*, I, 197–210)

With the earth above and the waters below, this scene resembles the natural setting in the theatre in 'Home in Grasmere', or the concluding moments of the revelation of imagination's landscape atop Mount Snowdon in *The Prelude*. Once again earth, sky, and water are transformed by the travelling light of the sun into an image manifesting the presence of the divine. The natural world is elided and becomes the radiant image of the divine; the appearances of nature become the point of mediation between the finite and the eternal. The natural poet responds in 'such access of mind'[25] that, 'Thought was not',[26] and there remains only the purely visionary apprehension of the divine manifest in the sparkling images before him, whose being is sheer appearance.

In 'An Unpublished Tour' there is a prose explicitation of this descent of the holy upon earth:

And what a (?pensive) radiance is afar off upon the distance, what a solemnity & majesty of the departed sun glowing upon the crags and on the turf of those lofty mountains, a (?twilight illumination), an abated splendour! We recognize it as a bequest of the (departed) sun which ripens (the) harvest of the earth and guides its restless Inhabitant thro' the round of his daily occupations. Yet in the bedarkened recess

[24] *The Excursion*, I, 212.
[25] Ibid., I, 211.
[26] Ibid., I, 213.

from which this remote glory is distinctly beheld, the Spectator is touched by the sight—as it were a descent of something heavenly upon earth, vouchsafed to aid his imagination in determining the texture of the everlasting regions & what kind of substance it is which the feet of angels tread upon . . .[27]

The scene here is once again Grasmere, and though there is something of the fanciful and the picturesque in Wordsworth's tone toward the reader as he leads him into the vale, there is a serious undertone to what is being said. It lacks the intensity of the passages we have been looking at, but the memory of the moments contained in them seems to lie just below the surface, as though the natural scene were about to undergo a transformation once again.

In 'Strange fits of passion have I known', there is an uncanny and unconscious communion between the soul of the rider under the moon and its movement in the sky.[28] A similar unconscious communion with the moon's light is described in Book I of *The Prelude*. The natural setting is the Sands of Westmoreland, which become under the moon's influence a field of light where the ten-year-old Wordsworth stands a stranger to it, yet feeding unconsciously upon it like a 'bee among the Flowers'.[29] The boy is drawn to the light, yet he has 'no conscious memory of a kindred sight'.[30] For the grown man, however, looking back upon the scene in recollection, the unconscious significance of the child's intercourse with the field of light becomes conscious in the recognition that it was a communion with 'the eternal Beauty':

> Yes, I remember, when the changeful earth,
> And twice five seasons on my mind had stamp'd
> The faces of the moving year, even then,

[27] *Pr.W.*, vol. ii, p. 313.

[28] Cf. the interplay of inner and outer illumination in this passage from 'Home at Grasmere':

> 　　　　　　　. . . but yet to me I feel
> That an internal brightness is vouchsafed
> That must not die, that must not pass away.
> Why does this inward lustre fondly seek,
> And gladly blend with outward fellowship?
> Why do *they* shine around me whom I love?
> 　　　　　　　　　　　(674–9)

in *PW.*, vol. v.

[29] *The Prelude*, I, 608.
[30] Ibid., I, 602.

A Child, I held unconscious intercourse
With the eternal Beauty, drinking in
A pure organic pleasure from the lines
Of curling mist, or from the level plain
Of waters colour'd by the steady clouds.

(*Prelude*, I, 586–93)

The significance of what is seen is recovered in recollection and the transfigured field of light is recognized as a representative, intermediary scene in which the 'first-born' affinities of the mind to its world are formed. But the true dimensions of this scene, touching upon the vast compass of the visionary, remain unspeakable. In the image of eternity generated by the metaphor of light the conscious significance of the experience of the eternal is embedded. Wordsworth does not attempt to render in verse the visionary experience alone, but to articulate the vision of the eternal in the appearances of nature as it is accompanied by its significance. The experience of the holy is a purely visionary moment from which interpretation is absent. In recollection the significance of that experience is disclosed, and becomes either the medium of its representation, or is placed to the side as a frame within which the experience is presented.

The metaphors of eternity in Wordsworth's poetry are composed of figures washed up on the banks of memory after the flood of the imagination has passed.[31] The act of recollection

---

31 In both *The Excursion*, VII, 25–30, and *The Prelude*, VI, 540–8, the presence of the imagination in an access of mind is seen as a flooding over which leaves behind it in memory the traces of its presence:

And, when the stream
Which overflowed the soul was passed away,
A consciousness remained that it had left,
Deposited upon the silent shore
Of memory, images and precious thoughts
That shall not die, and cannot be destroyed.

(*Excursion*)

With hope it is, hope that can never die,
Effort, and expectation, and desire,
And something evermore about to be.
The mind beneath such banners militant
Thinks not of spoils or trophies, nor of aught
That may attest its prowess, blest in thoughts
That are their own perfection and reward,
Strong in itself, and in the access of joy
Which hides it like the overflowing Nile.

(*Prelude*)

recovers the significance of what was revealed in the visitation of the imagination, and the poet forms from what is left after the passage of the imagination the sign which points, like a covenant, backward to what has happened, and forward toward what may come again, and beyond that into eternity, 'what is evermore about to be'.

The metaphor for eternity generates an image from which the eternal may be intimated. Its ground is in what the imagination reveals. The accidental appearances of nature are coincident with an internal state, an 'access of mind', and become the seeds sown in a celestial soil which recollection harvests. It is the act of recollection, utimately, which determines the precise configuration of the metaphors of eternity. They are, to borrow and modify an image from Nietzsche, like comets landed upon earth, still bearing the aura of having come from out of the unknown.

The metaphor for eternity appears as a genetic form in Wordsworth. Birth and generation are the dominant modes in which the relationship between the finite and the eternal is seen. For Wordsworth they form a part of what seems to be an organic chain linking the soul of the poet, the natural world, and the holy which is present in their union. In the creative act of the imagination the advent of this metaphor is represented through images of organic generation and growth. A genetic metaphor is intended to represent a genetic act; the act intends its representation and discovers itself in it. Trope and act, metaphor and origin, imagination and recollection are implicated in a genetic process whose representation seemingly has its ground in the realm of natural analogy. But the metaphor for eternity is an extreme case, where the operation of natural analogy fades away, is even erased, as is the natural scene in the presence of the holy, or as the star/soul is separated from its orbit. And it is at this point, where the genetic metaphor turns back on itself, seed within seed, that the organic relation to nature begins to break down under the pressure of the imagination.

CHAPTER III

A Prospect in My Mind:
Growing up a Poet
(A Chapter of Images)

Ein Rätsel ist Reinentsprungenes. Auch
Der Gesang kaum darf es enthüllen. Denn
Wie du anfingst, wirst du bleiben
So viel auch wirket die Not,
Und die Zucht, das meiste nämlich
Vermag die Geburt,
Und der Lichtstrahl, der
Dem Neugebornen begegnet.
Wo aber ist einer,
Um frei zu bleiben
Sein Leben lang, und des Herzens Wunsch
Allein zu erfüllen, so
Aus günstigen Höhn, wie der Rhein,
Und so aus heiligem Schosse
Glücklich geboren, wie jener?

'Der Rhein', HÖLDERLIN

In looking at the objects of Nature while I am think-
ing, as at yonder moon dim-glimmering through the
dewy windowpane, I seem rather to be seeking, as it
were *asking*, a symbolic language for something with-
in me that already and forever exists, than observing
anything new. Even when that latter is the case, yet I
still have always an obscure feeling as if that new
phaenomenon were the dim Awaking of a forgotten
or hidden Truth of my inner Nature. It is still interest-
ing as a Word a Symbol.

COLERIDGE: *Notebooks*, 14 April 1805

[I]

WORDSWORTH had, he said, from the very first two natures, 'joy
the one/The other melancholy'.[1] They mark, roughly, the line
dividing from one another the two dominant interpretive views
of Wordsworth's representation of the way he grew to become a
poet. The first of these, the 'melancholy', but also the more tradi-
tional, derives its perspective principally from 'Tintern Abbey'
and the 'Intimations Ode'. It regards the growth of Wordsworth's
poetic powers from the point of view of their final alteration and
decline. The development of the poet is articulated as a series of
transformations beginning in infancy, moving through the 'stages'
of childhood, youth, and early manhood, and culminating in a
mastery of a poetic power all toó quickly afflicted with 'a sense of
inward decay that affects not however the natural life'.[2] This line
of interpretation concerns itself with the causes of the diminish-
ment of the poet's powers (which are various, and all speculative);
and, more importantly, with the more difficult problem of their
conversion into the 'philosophic mind',[3] or an ethics of survival:

In the Hawkshead poems we find the assumptions about the growth
of the individual mind that dominate his career: that the normal course
of human life involves a crisis of transition from naturalism to an
orthodox dualism; that this crisis threatens spiritual and psychological
decay; and that the task of man and poet is to survive it, to relinquish
youthful vision without loss of hope.[4]

A happier reading of the meaning of the growth of the poet's
mind derives its main argument from Wordsworth's representa-
tion of its complex processes in *The Prelude*. Chronologically it is
a more restricted view of his development, but a richer, more
ample one than the traditional precisely because of its conscious
limitations. The soul of the poet, as Robert Langbaum argues it in
'The Evolution of Soul in Wordsworth's Poetry', evolves in this
world through its experience of it: 'And it is the main purport of
Wordsworth's poetry to show the spiritual significance of this

1 *The Prelude*, X, 869–70.
2 'Reply to "Mathetes"', in *Pr.W.*, vol. II, p. 17.
3 Lionel Trilling, 'The Immortality Ode', in *The Liberal Imagination* (New York,
1950).
4 Paul D. Sheats, *The Making of Wordsworth's Poetry, 1785–1798* (Cambridge, 1973),
p. 33.

world, to show that we evolve a soul or identity through experi-
ence and that the very process of evolution is what we mean by
soul'.[5] As it progresses in life the soul, by constant recurrence in
memory to its beginnings, forms the bonds uniting its past to its
present. This conscious regression in memory determines the
configuration of the soul and the relation of the self to the
natural world:

> Place, in Wordsworth, is the spatial projection of psyche, because it is
> the repository of memory. We can understand the relation in Words-
> worth between mind and nature, once we understand that Wordsworth
> evolves his soul or sense of identity as he identifies more and more
> such hallowed places. We can understand the relation in Wordsworth
> between the themes of memory and growing up, once we understand
> that for Wordsworth you advance in life by travelling back again to the
> beginning, by reassessing your life, by binding your days together
> anew.[6]

In such evolution nothing is lost. As Mr Langbaum reads it,
Wordsworth's response to the question concerning the adult's
sense of loss posed by the 'Intimations Ode' is to say, '. . . that
nothing is lost. Even if we no longer experience the "glory" we
experienced in childhood, "nature yet remembers." Our souls,
he concludes in a strikingly primitivist image, can in a moment
travel backward'.[7] The end of the soul's evolution lies in its
beginning, in never letting it go, even though it remains only as
something remembered. Yet to say that nothing is lost because it
is remembered is to obscure the distinction between experience
and recollection, which is necessary for us if we are to com-
prehend what Wordsworth means when he does speak of a loss
of power, of a fading away of an inner light. Mr Langbaum is, I
think, correct to assert that for Wordsworth everything he is sur-
vives the successive turns in the path of his development; but it
survives as something altered and diminished in power, though
augmented in value.[8]

[5] Robert Langbaum, 'The Evolution of Soul in Wordsworth's Poetry', in *The Modern Spirit: Essays on the Continuity of Nineteenth- and Twentieth-Century Literature* (New York, 1970), p. 18.

[6] Ibid., p. 33.

[7] Ibid., p. 22.

[8] Geoffrey Hartman in his chapter on the *via naturaliter negativa* (*Wordsworth's Poetry 1787–1814*, pp. 33–69) makes a similar, even homeomorphic, argument for an optimistic view of Wordsworth's development.

These two quite different conceptions of Wordsworth's repre-
sentation of the growth of his mind are not, in theory at least,
exclusive of one another. My concern in this chapter is not with
their similarity, but, rather, with what the divergence between
them indicates: the possibility of interpreting the development of
Wordsworth's poetic mind both ways simultaneously, of seeing,
that is, in the decay of his powers the condition which made poetic
creation possible. To read him in this way we must begin by
understanding the links among the privileged position with which
Wordsworth invests the child newly come into the world, the
decay of his inner power, and his perception of this declining
power as imagination. The end of his growth as a poet lies in the
consummation of the imaginative union of mind and nature,
'where hope and memory are as one',[9] which is the image of
poetry for Wordsworth. When seen in relation to its beginnings,
the end or aim of his development becomes intelligible, and,
therefore, a source of power for him. However obscure his begin-
nings might be for the poet, it is his obsession with the attempt
to articulate them, to make them conscious, that makes effective
the power of his poetic nature. In what he discovers of himself
through recollection of the progression of his life lies the power
to bring to rest the 'wavering balance' of his mind, and induce
those calm moods in which Wordsworth felt most himself.

The child retains an awful, divine, and yet puzzlingly fragile
power for a short time after its birth. Then it begins to wane, to
become 'a sleep and a forgetting', and as it fades, extinction
threatens it through the presence and pressure of the external
world oppressively manifest to it most immediately and power-
fully in the despotic influence of the eye:

> The state to which I now allude was one
> In which the eye was master of the heart,
> When that which is in every stage of life
> The most despotic of our senses gain'd
> Such strength in me as often held my mind
> In absolute dominion.
>
> > (*Prelude*, XI, 171–6)

The mind held in 'absolute dominion' by the eye is in a state
oposite to that of the infant in the 'Intimations Ode', who from

---

[9] 'The Tuft of Primroses', *PW.*, vol. v, l. 292.

its 'being's height' holds sway over the dimly perceived world in which it finds itself. But as the power of its internal being begins to wane, it begins to perceive the external world more clearly. From this point on the links shaped through the sensual apprehension of the external world will begin to form the bonds impounding the mind within the natural world. And it is against the force and pressure of the senses that the mind must struggle to preserve its own inner being, and only in so far as it can preserve it, will it be able to remain free from a slavery to the senses that would be its death.

Growing up seems, to the poet recollecting that progressive journey, to be dependent upon the waning of the divine power manifest in the soul of the child, for only its abatement allows the child to form its initial ties with the natural world. The inward decay of this power is one primary sense of what growth means to Wordsworth; the other such meaning it has for him is presented through the development and elaboration of the child's first filial bonds with the natural world into a complex structure of images and comprehended relationships which becomes what he calls a 'language of the sense', in 'Tintern Abbey'. The origin of these bonds, as we shall see in detail later, remains concealed. The character of this sensible structure of the mind is represented both in terms of the loving bond between mother and child in Book II of *The Prelude*, and as the subtle, dark forging of a chain which nature uses to entrap and betray the mind. It is not so much to the natural world as such that the divine power of the child's soul must accommodate itself, as to the syntax of the logic which the senses speak to the soul, and, in speaking, build up into the structure of a natural mind through habit, custom, and repetition. As this 'interminable building' of the senses rises up to become the natural mind, the inner being of the poet (especially as he represents it in *The Prelude*) becomes like a wild, untamed creature treacherously yoked to a burden it does not wish to bear, and from which it cannot escape. The soul must uneasily learn ways to accommodate itself to its imprisonment:

> . . . and in that dubious hour,
> That twilight when we first begin to see
> This dawning earth, to recognize, expect;
> And in the long probation that ensues,
> The time of trial, ere we learn to live

> In reconcilement with our stinted powers,
> To endure this state of meagre vassalage;
> Unwilling to forego, confess, submit,
> Uneasy and unsettled, yoke-fellows
> To custom, mettlesome, and not yet tam'd
> And humbled down, oh! then we feel, we feel,
> We know when we have Friends.
>
>   (*Prelude*, V, 536–47)

These friends are fairy-tales. In them the child finds a world intermediate between the divine one from which it has come and the earthly one which restrains it. Fairy-tales mediate between the soul of the child and the natural world, and form a passage through which the soul may pass from one world to the other. Their mediation makes somewhat easier the reconcilement of the soul to its earthly privations.

The divine power of the child, awesome as it is for Wordsworth, endures in the oppression of 'the laws of vulgar sense'[10] the threat that the structures of mind built up by the logic of perception will form a false nature, a 'universe of death',[11] forcefully suppressing the real nature of the mind residing in the decaying power of an immortal soul. Neither 'nature' can bear the other's immediate presence, for each is the negation of the other. Their relationship must be a mediated one. In the act of recollection Wordsworth found the form which such mediation could take in his poetry; he discovered in recollection what he would forget when pulled into the busy vortex of the senses—that his inner being was immortal and infinite. From that discovery came his freedom from a slavery to the senses, and the power to subject the external world to the workings of the imagination.[12] Wordsworthy's study of the growth of his own mind was to be a prelude to a long philosophic poem on the nature of man. But to write that poem he felt that he first must know the character of his own poetic power, for in such knowledge lay his power.

---

[10] *The Prelude*, XIII, 140.

[11] Ibid., 141.

[12] The relation of imagination to the senses in Wordsworth resembles that worked out by Kant in his *Critique of Judgment*. The former is not derivable from the latter, in my opinion, but their resemblance could make the focus of another study which would attempt to bring together coherently what we can know about the development of the idea of the imagination.

The source of his power as a poet lay in the recognition, proceeding from recollection, of the significance of the divine, but decaying, light of the mind. This power could become efficacious only if it could be freed from the prison-house of the senses, if, through a counterpoised separation, a conscious balance between the two natures within him could be formed:

> . . . for the mind
> Learns from such timely exercise to keep
> In wholesome separation the two natures,
> The one that feels, the other that observes.
> (*Prelude*, XIII, 328–31)

The act of recollection informing the structure of *The Prelude* liberates the poet from his entrapment in the present moment and from the tyranny of the immediate pressure of the senses by allowing the power of the imagination to emerge and reassert itself as a consciousness of the mind's absolute dominion in the presence of the natural world. Nature ceases to threaten to extinguish the soul's divine light, and becomes, in time, a sensible language. As such, however, this language remains ambiguous, for it not only constitutes the linkage of the soul's earthly yoke, the sign of its stinted powers, but it becomes in time the language through whose temporally articulated syntax the poet interprets himself to himself. In discovering the power of his mind through, yet over against, a sensible nature, Wordsworth comes to know that from his immortal being flows the power of his imagination. Through his growing natural finitude he learns to recognize his abiding, immortal infinitude.

If we are, then, to understand the meaning of the growth of the mind of the poet through the declining power of his soul, we must begin with the way Wordsworth represents the divine power of the inner being of the child just come into this world from another. The growth of the child is made intelligible through the narration of what happens to that power as it is affected by the senses. That power suffers alteration; the anamnestic shadow under which the child in the 'Intimations Ode' moves, seeing in nature a glory cast by its mind's unconscious powers, becomes, with its decay, the power of imagination. It is the power of the mind to preserve, relatively, itself; to remain immortally alive

through the recollective recognition of its origin in what trans-
cends nature. In this rests the capacity of the soul to resist the
pressure of the senses to annihilate it: 'But the Imagination is
conscious of an indestructible dominion;—the Soul may fall away
from it, not being able to sustain its grandeur; but, if once felt
and acknowledged, by no act of any other faculty of the mind can
it be relaxed, impaired, or diminished'.[13] The growth of the poet
leads toward this conscious act of the imagination. How it does
so remains to be set out.

[11]

Upon entering the world the infant is both 'deaf and silent'.[14]
Enclosed within the simple 'cloud of infancy'[15] it communes with
its own internal, immortal being as a reader of the 'eternal deep'.[16]
Inwardly absorbed, the child neither sees nor hears the world out-
side itself. He passes his first days on earth within the sphere of
his own self-absorbed oblivion. If there were nothing to violate
the equilibrium of that sphere the child would remain wrapped
in it, never knowing as it grew the character of the external world.
Yet once violated, the sphere of the infant's inner world rapidly
starts to empty, to pour itself out, as the bond with the natural
world, once formed, begins with amazing speed and power to
augment itself and to encroach in a not often pleasant way upon
the space of the child's internal being. What the precise nature of
this violation of the inner life of the child is remains unspoken
in the 'Intimations Ode', and is represented as something mysteri-
ous and unintelligible in *The Prelude*.

> Thou little Child, yet glorious in the might
> Of heaven-born freedom on thy being's height,
> Why with such earnest pains dost thou provoke
> The years to bring the inevitable yoke,
> Thus blindly with thy blessedness at strife?
> ('Intimations Ode', 125–9)

The child's provocation of time is not presented as an explanation

13 'Preface to the Edition of 1815', *Pr.W.*, vol. III, pp. 36–7.
14 'Intimations Ode', l. 112.
15 *The Excursion*, IV, 83–6.
16 'Intimations Ode', l. 112.

for its fall into the world, but as an act whose motivation remains
concealed.

It is, perhaps, the giddy and unstable height from which the
child views his world which induces in him the playful, provoca-
tive mood leading to his fall. Somewhat like Heraclitus' child who
builds and rebuilds the universe as his game, Wordsworth's infant
plays with its dreamlike world until it is yoked to it by the real
presence of its fantasies. It is in fairy-tales that the child discovers
a world like its own where time and space are responsive to its
wishes and commands:

> Ye dreamers, then,
> Forgers of lawless tales! we bless you then,
> Impostors, drivellers, dotards, as the ape
> Philosophy will call you: then we feel
> With what, and how great might ye are in league,
> Who make our wish our power, our thought a deed,
> An empire, a possession; Ye whom Time
> And Seasons serve; all Faculties; to whom
> Earth crouches, th' elements are potter's clay,
> Space like a Heaven fill'd up with Northern lights;
> Here, nowhere, there, and everywhere at once.
>
> (*Prelude*, V, 547–57)

Like young Malte, in Rilke's *Notebooks of Malte Laurids Brigge*,
who was trapped behind the mask he had put on to act out a part
of life taken from the adult world, Wordsworth's child is drawn
into the external world because it is for him a game; but once in
the world he finds that he is bound to it and 'cannot untwist the
links by which, in no undelightful harmony, images and senti-
ments are wedded in his mind'.[17]

The point of union where the inner world of sentiment is
wedded to the natural world of powerful presences remains hid-
den. And for, it seems, good reason. Though the two worlds are
'intertwined' and form together the framework of the growing
mind, they do not have a single origin, but separate ones counter-
posed to one another. The familiar metaphors Wordsworth uses
to represent the 'marriage' of the inner world to the outer are
those which have to do with planting and grafting, with streams
flowing into one another and with transpositions from one sphere

17 'Reply to "Mathetes"', *Pr.W.*, vol. iii, p. 16.

to another.[18] These images render manifest the bonding of two
separate entities whose union is never total, and never forms a
third entity essentially unlike the first two. Inner and outer
worlds mutually affect one another, as we shall see, yet neither is
affected in its essential core. They remain separate in their union,
beings of two different ontological orders; each one is potentially
the negator or destroyer of the other:

> Nature will either end thee quite;
> Or, lengthening out thy season of delight,
> Preserve for thee, by individual right,
> A young lamb's heart among the fullgrown flocks.
> ('To H. C. Six Years Old', 21–4)

The infant rests upon its 'being's height' surrounded by the
nimbus of the awful might of its soul. In *The Prelude* Wordsworth
names this height a throne and perceives it as the location of the
simplicity of childhood:

> . . . our childhood sits,
> Our simple childhood sits upon a throne
> That hath more power than all the elements.
> I guess not what this tells of Being past,
> Nor what it augurs of the life to come;
> But so it is;
>
> (*Prelude*, V, 531–6)

And in *The Excursion* it is with the child's simplicity that God
communes:

> —thou, who didst wrap the cloud
> Of infancy around us, that thyself,
> Therein, with our simplicity awhile
> Might'st hold, on earth, communion undisturbed;
> (*Excursion*, IV, 83–6)

The child's simplicity, its single inner being, permits this silent,
direct intercourse with the divine. Wordsworth's images for this
simplicity are those of elemental fire and water. These embody,
without making intelligible, the initial internal movement of the
soul toward the external world through which the simplicity of
the child's mind becomes the scattered complexity of the adult's

[18] See the diverse metaphors of growth and intertwining in the following passages
in *The Prelude*: I, 305–6; 428–41; 586–608; II, 203–37.

consciousness. In 'Home at Grasmere' the mind of the poet is
seen as an internal brightness which perceives and is drawn to
glowing presences beyond itself:

> . . . but yet to me I feel
> That an internal brightness is vouchsafed
> That must not die, that must not pass away.
> Why does this inward lustre fondly seek,
> And gladly blend with outward fellowship?
> Why do *they* shine around me whom I love?
> Why do they teach me whom I thus revere?
> Strange question, yet it answers not itself.[19]

Again, as so often elsewhere, the origin of the movement of the
soul towards the external world is presented as a question for
which there is no forthcoming answer.

In 'To H. C. Six Years Old' the child is a 'faery voyager' upon
the clear waters of its inner being:

> O THOU! whose fancies from afar are brought;
> Who of thy words dost make a mock apparel,
> And fittest to unutterable thought
> The breeze-like motion and the self-born carol;
> Thou faery voyager! that dost float
> In such clear water, that thy boat
> May rather seem
> To brood on air than on an earthly stream;
> Suspended in a stream as clear as sky,
> Where earth and heaven do make one imagery;
> O blessèd vision! happy child!
>
> (1–11)

Heaven and earth make one image in the limpid simplicity of the
child's soul. Yet it is a fragile state; it hangs 'a dewdrop, which the
morn brings forth', 'A gem that glitters', and can slip 'in a
moment out of life'.

One of the most startling of Wordsworth's metaphors for the
violation of the child's simplicity is in Book IV of *The Prelude*:

> Whatever shadings of mortality
> Had fallen upon these objects heretofore
> Were different in kind; not tender: strong,

---

[19] 'Home at Grasmere', *PW.*, vol. v, Appendix A, pp. 335–6, ll. 674–81. Cf. also
The Excursion, IV, 50.

> Deep, gloomy were they and severe; the scatterings
> Of Childhood;
>
>   (*Prelude*, IV, 240–4)

These intimations of mortality scatter the cloud of simple infancy; it becomes rain, and falls wildly like the rushing water of a mountain stream down from its heights. 'Home at Grasmere' presents the fall of the turbulent soul of the child into nature, where it is tamed, as the descent of a mountain stream to the plain below it:

> But me hath Nature tamed, and bade to seek
> For other agitations, or be calm;
> Hath dealt with me as with a turbulent Stream,
> Some nursling of the mountains, whom she leads
> Through quiet meadows, after he has learnt
> His strength, and had his triumph and his joy
> His desperate course of tumult and of glee.
> That which in stealth by Nature was performed
> Hath Reason sanctioned.[20]

Having moved beyond the self-containment of its inner sphere the soul becomes a wild thing to be yoked and tamed by nature. And once in nature, the soul must learn to live with stinted powers. What binds the soul to nature, and eventually reconciles it to its vassalage there is the growth of the framework of the poet's natural mind which is built up out of his experience of the natural world. Upon the limpid river of his mind the faery voyager sails out into the world beyond himself. His simple being becomes the foundation for a complex structure of sense experiences which forms the banks through which the infinite soul of the child flows reluctantly into its finite world. The way in which the formation of this structure of the natural mind is initiated remains hidden from the poet, and is something whose nature is not revealed to him through the images he uses to indicate its nature, for its foundation rests upon the divine nature of the soul, which is concealed, in turn, by that structure. The ground from which the framework of the natural mind rises remains hidden from view and inarticulable. It is easily forgotten, and when it is the mind of the poet, no longer conscious of the power of its divine internal being, falls prey to the despotism of the busy vortex of sensual

---

[20] 'Home at Grasmere', ll. 726–34.

experience. Yet in privileged moments, which occur throughout *The Prelude*, it is recalled to itself, and becomes conscious of its freedom from oppression of the senses.

[III]

If there is a fear present at times in Worldsworth's poetry that the mind will annihilate its bond with nature, there is an equally great fear that nature will extinguish the soul of the poet. The soul's existence, once in nature, is contested by it. Nature exists for the growing child only in so far as it is a thing of the senses; it communicates with him through the eye and ear; he reads and yet defies its commands; it is both joy and terror to him; it dazzles him with the tumult of emotions it sets in motion. His earliest response to nature is a kind of wild joy, an uncontrolled, imitative dance before the multiplicity of things in motion outside himself. This tumult, Wordsworth says, is gradually tamed through the agencies of fear and the loving delight he took in finding an order in nature by discovering the hidden relations among natural objects.

The taming of the soul of the child, its gradual accommodation to a natural, finite world is not without violence to both the soul and to nature. There are moments in Wordsworth's poetry when the child attacks nature with an open violence, as in 'Nutting', and others where this violence is more covert, manifesting itself in acts of theft (of a boat, of another's snares). A feeling of guilt succeeds these moments, arising not so much from a sense of having committed a moral trespass, as from a dim awareness of an alienation from nature, of being other than it, which the violence of the child's plundering and thieving discloses to it. It unleashes in him powers whose enormous force he had not reckoned on; they reveal to him in the starkest manner his otherness, as in the days following the theft of the shepherd's boat moored on the shore of Ullswater:

> . . . and after I had seen
> That spectacle, for many days, my brain
> Work'd with a dim and undetermin'd sense
> Of unknown modes of being; in my thoughts
> There was a darkness, call it solitude,

> Or blank desertion, no familiar shapes
> Of hourly objects, images of trees,
> Of sea or sky, no colours of green fields;
> But huge and mighty Forms that do not live
> Like living men mov'd slowly through the mind
> By day and were the trouble of my dreams.
>   (*Prelude*, I, 417–27)

The child's audacious attack upon nature's restraining presence lacks a clear motive; his violence reveals dimly to him the awful presences lurking within his soul. Yet they are only partially disclosed to the child, for he does not see in them a causal link with his violent action, but perceives them simply as a result of it. They were not there before he acted, only afterward. What he did in some sense summoned them. But the child does not perceive them as the motive source of his actions. The adult looking back upon these scenes of violence glimpses in them the resistance of his own soul to its natural servitude.

Counterbalancing the shattering effect of violence upon the child's bond with nature is the power of love travelling through the gaze of the mother to the child feeding at her breast. Love's agency informs the child's acts of perception and enables the augmentation of his 'infant sensibility' through the discovery of the concealed kinship of natural things. Love makes such seeing possible, and from it is built the framework of the child's natural mind, which, as it rises up, becomes the yoke taming the soul to its earthly vassalage.

> What wonder if I speak
> With fervour, am exalted with the thought
> Of my possessions, of my genuine wealth
> Inward and outward, what I keep, have gain'd,
> Shall gain, must gain, if sound be my belief
> From past and present, rightly understood,
> That in my day of Childhood I was less
> The mind of Nature, less, take all in all,
> Whatever may be lost, than I am now.[21]

The sensible augmentation of the natural mind is an event whose processes constitute a poetic inversion of St. Paul's remarks in I Corinthians 15 concerning the sowing of the earthly body which

----

[21] Ibid., MS B, pp. 315–16.

is raised a spiritual body.[22] Wordsworth's poet's soul is sown a spiritual power which is raised a natural body. Yet the ground in which this seed is sown, and upon which the 'interminable building' of the natural mind arises, remains hidden. Strictly speaking, Wordsworth says, the mind has no beginning:

> But who shall parcel out
> His intellect, by geometric rules,
> Split, like a province, into round and square?
> Who knows the individual hour in which
> His habits were first sown, even as a seed,
> Who that shall point, as with a wand, and say,
> 'This portion of the river of my mind
> Came from yon fountain?'
>
> .   .   .   .
>
> Hard task to analyse a soul, in which,
> Not only general habits and desires,
> But each most obvious and particular thought,
> Not in a mystical and idle sense,
> But in the words of reason deeply weigh'd,
> Hath no beginning.
>
> (*Prelude*, II, 208–37)

The natural mind is grasped by the poet, in an act of recollection, as a project already under way, as a journey already begun whose end must be intimated from the path he has travelled. Already in the world, and open to it, the mind of the child is sustained in its early intercourse with nature by its mother's love. But when that prop was removed from the incomplete structure of the mind at her death:

> I was left alone,
> Seeking the visible world, nor knowing why.
> The props of my affection were remov'd,
> And yet the building stood, as if sustain'd
> By its own spirit!
>
> (*Prelude*, II, 292–6)

---

[22] St. Paul, I Corinthians 15 : 42–4: 'So is it with the resurrection of the dead. What is sown is perishable, what is raised is imperishable. It is sown in dishonour, it is raised in glory. It is sown in weakness, it is raised in power. It is sown a physical body, it is raised a spiritual body.' The logic of this is not far removed from Socrates' defence of the immortality of the soul in the *Phaedo*, or from the doctrine of anamnesis which underlies it.

The mind of the child seeks the 'visible world' beyond itself. It does this on its own, yet why it does so is never made clear. The beginnings of this process by which the building of the natural mind is constructed are never disclosed, and they cannot serve, consequently, as a means of explaining the attraction of the natural world for the young child. This attraction is perceived only as a process already in motion at the earliest moments the poet can remember.

If the origin of the natural mind cannot serve as the ground for interpreting the meaning of its development, then no single way of explaining the nature of this process, or of representing it, offers itself to the poet. The formation of the natural mind becomes, therefore, a process open to different interpretations and representations at different stages in its development. The yoke and vassalage of the senses in early childhood become the wild delight of the boy running free in wood and meadow, and this in turn is subdued and transformed into a calmer pleasure by the discovery that nature feels in sympathy with the soul, like a sea mirroring its inner life. There is, as Wordsworth represents it in *The Prelude*, an accommodating progress of the mind by which the 'mighty' soul of the child passes from out of its anamnestic oblivion toward conscious recognition of itself, of its destiny and powers, by discovering in nature the means of interpreting itself to itself. This passage from obliviousness to a recognition of the soul's dominion over itself, from an experience of the natural world as silent and without meaning toward the disclosure of the meaning of that silence in a natural language, is made through a series of stages, of mediations performed by nature, man, and books, though in no particular order, or hierarchy, and leading the child to a discovery of its natural finitude. The finite mind, the 'mind of nature', prepares, as it grows, the ground upon which the revelation of the soul's infinitude becomes possible. It is over against nature, against the encroachment of the finite structure of the natural mind, that the poet discovers, in the consciousness of an absolute freedom and power within himself, the way to subordinate the activity of the senses to the divine nature of his internal being. Such moments of conscious awareness Wordsworth calls the visitations of the imagination. In preserving its dominion and asserting its power over the natural mind, the soul comes to know the conscious power of its internal preservation as imagination. The growth of the structure of the natural mind entails the conversion of the anamnestic shadow which encloses the infant into the intervenient visitations of the imagination. These visitations are repetitions in the life of the adult of the shadowy world seen by the child.

The development of the poet's mind from infancy to the time recorded at the end of *The Prelude* is linked to the reciprocating interplay of the soul and the natural and historical world which it encounters. Once the soul has begun to develop in nature, there is a double movement to its growth in *The Prelude*: there is, first, the raising up of an 'above ground' framework built by the logic of perception over an abyss with no bottom:

> ... for I had an eye
> Which in my strongest workings, evermore
> Was looking for the shades of difference
> As they lie hid in all exterior forms,
> Near or remote, minute or vast, an eye
> Which from a stone, a tree, a wither'd leaf,
> To the broad ocean and the azure heavens,
> Spangled with kindred multitudes of stars,
> Could find no surface where its power might sleep,
> Which spake perpetual logic to my soul,
> And by an unrelenting agency
> Did bind my feelings, even as in a chain.
>
> (*Prelude*, III, 156–67)

And, second, there is an abiding, yet separate, presence in the power of the imagination flowing underground and emerging at propitious moments, transfiguring in its manifestation the dead letter of the eye's logic into the living word of the spirit.

The eye characterizes and dominates the interplay of the mind and the natural and historical worlds it comes to know. The effect upon his natural mind of what the poet sees becomes manifest in a logical and coherent structure of relations and interrelations. The eye has the power to absorb the poet in the perpetual motion of the present moment; he falls, if we may borrow an image from Ernst Bloch's *Spüren*, into the trap of the present,[23] and is swept along by it, overwhelmed often and tyrannized by the images of the external world which press in upon him. In his youth, Words-

---

[23] Quoted in Louis Marin, 'Remarques critiques sur l'énonciation: La question du présent dans le discours', *MLN*, vol. xci, No. 5, pp. 945–6.

worth says, he was never free from the oppression of the senses. Caught up in the vortex of the present moment, lacking real direction and purpose, floating in search of one or the other, or both, the eye falls unsteadily upon its object. So Wordsworth appears to himself, floating upon the current of a sudden inspiration, in the opening lines of *The Prelude*. He is not, he says, used to making the present moment the object of his song, and he allows the spontaneous moment to follow its course. When it has passed, he sets off for a place where a more regular life and a more balanced mind will free him from a dependence upon the precarious and uncontrolled flux of the spontaneously present.

What the eye perceives becomes the chance acquisition of the occasion. There is no design in what the eye chooses to glance at, or not, and yet what it perceives builds up in the soul that interminable structure whose bricks are the images of external things impinging upon the senses, and whose mortar is the logic which the act of perception speaks to the soul. From the hazards of random perception, and from their accidental repetition arises the 'mansion' of custom, tradition, and habit by which the awful tumult of the poet's soul is tamed. By the mediation of nature, gradually becoming a language of the sense, the mind of the poet is reconciled to its stinted powers. Beginning first with an attraction, which becomes habitual, toward the things in nature most like itself in power (the sun, for the way it touched the earth, was Wordsworth's first natural love), the soul in time accustoms itself to value, esteem even, what is less grand in nature, and to proceed from there toward a love of man. Yet this progression through a series of mediated stages from the sublime to the beautiful in nature, to the human and ethical, though it appears in the retrospective prospect articulated by recollection to be an orderly and reasonable progression down through the stages of a natural hierarchy, is, the poet says repeatedly, a fortunate accident. What he has become, the construction of his finite, natural self, is the result of sheer chance, the most important aspect of that being the great good luck he had to be raised and educated in the Lake Country:

> Yet in the midst
> Of these vagaries, with an eye so rich
> As mine was, through the chance, on me not wasted

Of having been brought up in such a grand
And lovely region, I had forms distinct
To steady me; these thoughts did oft revolve
About some centre palpable, which at once
Incited them to motion, and control'd,
And whatsoever shape the fit might take,
And whencesoever it might come, I still
At all times had a real solid world
Of images about me; did not pine
As one in cities bred might do;
                    (*Prelude*, VIII, 593–605)

His self, his temporal identity as he might call it, is the successful survivor of its own accidents. The fall of the soul into nature is a happy accident, in the end.

But arriving at that end is no simple journey. Having been, in the Heideggerian sense, thrown into the world, the child, who will become a poet, discovers himself as already implicated in an intricate and oppressive fabric of relationships with the world about him. The adult must learn to master these relationships as his own willed and controlled choices before he can become a poet. His power as a poet is efficacious only when there is a space opened up for it to enter and occupy, a space opened up through the poet's conscious awareness of his mind's dominion over the logic of the eye and ear.

Wordsworth's metaphors for the growth of the framework of his natural mind are of two kinds: organic and architectonic. Neither kind represents, nor is meant to represent, the growth of the mind from its origins, but, rather, each renders manifest the processes of its development as a form of dynamic structuring. The natural mind is grasped by the poet as a presence already actively in motion, whose power and character he must come to know in order to make efficacious its relationship to the deeper, internal forces of the imagination. For Wordsworth these metaphors become a way of wielding the elements of his mind, of so articulating their relationship to one another as to release its imaginative powers. From the balance of these elements comes the freedom of the imagination to exercise its creative power. The natural mind is, accordingly, a fountain, a stream, a river; it is a seed whose growth becomes an intertwining of the passions with external objects; this intertwining is also represented as an engrafting of the beautiful forms of nature on to the mind. But these metaphors are mixed, at times indiscriminately, as in Book II of *The Prelude* (203–37), where the seed of habit is sown in the river of the mind. They do not proceed from a common source, but present, instead, differing partial views of the same process. In *The Prelude* the poet is moving toward a vision of the totality of that process and finds an efficacious image of the workings of his mind in the ascent of Mount Snowdon.

Organic metaphors articulate principally the bond between the natural mind and things in nature and embody, consequently, Wordsworth's sense of the linkage uniting the images peopling his mind. What is built up out of these organic linkages, however, is the 'mansion'[24] of the mind; a register of all permanent relations; a building with no beginning and no end, to which new rooms may always be added. The most telling of these architectonic images is music:

> The mind of Man is fram'd even like the breath
> And harmony of music. There is a dark
> Invisible workmanship that reconciles
> Discordant elements, and makes them move
> In one society. Ah me! that all
> The terrors, all the early miseries
> Regrets, vexations, lassitudes, that all
> The thoughts and feelings which have been infus'd
> Into my mind, should ever have made up
> The calm existence that is mine when I
> Am worthy of myself! Praise to the end!
> Thanks likewise for the means!
> (*Prelude*, I, 351–62)

That the harmonious structure of his natural being should arise out of such random and chance events seems to him mysterious and inexplicable. In the harmony of music coming from the discordant concordance of its elements Wordsworth found an adequate image for the 'dark workmanship' of his own mind. This image did not render that workmanship intelligible, but it did make it efficacious in making it manifest as an incomprehensible power. The tumult of his senses, moving in delight and terror before nature, is quieted in that mood of clear-sighted

---

[24] 'Tintern Abbey', l. 140; *The Prelude*, IV, 350.

harmony when he was most himself and could see most deeply into the nature of things. The 'calm existence' of which Wordsworth speaks here is a mood induced by the equipoise of all the accidental and occasional things which people the building of his mind. It is a mood which possesses him as much as he possesses it; it is a blessed mood, he says in 'Tintern Abbey', in which the power of harmony leads him on into the inner reaches of his own mind freeing him from the tyranny of the senses by laying them to sleep,

> . . . that blessed mood,
> In which the burthen of the mystery,
> In which the heavy and weary weight
> Of all this unintelligible world,
> Is lightened: —that serene and blessed mood
> In which the affections gently lead us on, —
> Until, the breath of this corporeal frame
> And even the motion of our human blood
> Almost suspended, we are laid asleep
> In body, and become a living soul:
> While with an eye made quiet by the power
> Of harmony, and the deep power of joy,
> We see into the life of things.
>
> ('Tintern Abbey', 37–49)

Wordsworth found in states like the one described above the link of exalted feeling, become mood, uniting the register of permenent relations constituting his natural mind with the inner light of the divine power of his soul, with, that is, the imagination. In this exalted mood the mind passes inward, beyond the oppressive framework of the natural mind toward a realization of the power of soul abiding beneath it and sustaining it.

Left to stand alone, without any connection with the imagination, the natural mind would become like a theatre where puppets act out a semblance of life which is no more than a living death:

> . . . that religious dignity of mind,
> That is the very faculty of truth;
> Which wanting, either, from the very first,
> A function never lighted up, or else
> Extinguish'd, Man, a creature great and good,
> Seems but a pageant plaything with vile claws

And this great frame of breathing elements
A senseless idol.

(*Prelude*, IV, 297–304)

In 'Essays upon Epitaphs, I', Wordsworth is more specific about
the necessity for maintaining a connection between the inner sense
of immortality a man carries with him and all that the senses
report to him of death, the most visible and dramatic image of his
finite and mortal nature:

We may, then, be justified in asserting, that the sense of immortality,
if not a co-existent and twin birth with Reason, is among the earliest of
her offspring: and we may further assert, that from these conjoined,
and under their countenance, the human affections are gradually
formed and opened out. This is not the place to enter into the recesses
of these investigations; but the subject requires me here to make a
plain avowal, that, for my own part, it is to me inconceivable, that the
sympathies of love towards each other, which grow with our growth,
could ever attain any new strength, or even preserve the old, after we
had received from the outward senses the impression of death, and
were in the habit of having that impression daily renewed and its
accompanying feeling brought home to ourselves, and to those we
love; if the same were not counteracted by those communications with
our internal Being, which are anterior to all these experiences, and with
which revelation coincides, and has through that coincidence alone
(for otherwise it could not possess it) a power to affect us. I confess, with
me the conviction is absolute, that, if the impression and sense of death
were not thus counterbalanced, such a hollowness would pervade the
whole system of things, such a want of correspondence and consistency,
a disproportion so astounding betwixt means and ends, that there
could be no repose, no joy.[25]

The communication 'with our internal Being' of which Words-
worth speaks coincides with revelation, for in this communication
the immortal nature of the soul is revealed. In his poetry of the
imagination the dominant mode of such communication lies in
those moods arising out of the temporary harmony of the struc-
ture of the natural mind and leading the poet, by virtue of the
power of that harmony, back into the interior realm of the mind
where the sources of his imaginative power lurk. There he dis-
covers the absolute dominion of his immortal soul.

[25] 'Essays upon Epitaphs, I', *Pr.W.*, vol. II, pp. 51–2.

From nature doth emotion come, and moods
Of calmness equally are nature's gift,
This is her glory;
(Prelude, XII, 1–3)

[IV]

In exalted feeling, in the calm mood induced by the contemplation of the 'sentiment of Being' spreading over everything that is in nature, Wordsworth discovered the connection between his 'two natures', the act uniting the framework of his natural mind to the sense of infinitude and power lurking within and beyond the reach of the finite part of his mind. From this union came a conscious knowledge of the power of the mind to subordinate the world of sense experience to an absolute, internal dominion, to see in the language of sense a revelation of divine power in the intimations of what lay beyond it:

> . . . I, at this time
> Saw blessings spread around me like a sea.
> Thus did my days pass on, and now at length
> From Nature and her overflowing soul
> I had receiv'd so much that all my thoughts
> Were steep'd in feeling; I was only then
> Contented when with bliss ineffable
> I felt the sentiment of Being spread
> O'er all that moves, and all that seemeth still,
> O'er all, that, lost beyond the reach of thought
> And human knowledge, to the human eye
> Invisible, yet liveth to the heart,
> O'er all that leaps, and runs, and shouts, and sings,
> Or beats the gladsome air, o'er all that glides
> Beneath the wave, yea, in the wave itself
> And mighty depth of waters. Wonder not
> If such my transports were; for in all things now
> I saw one life, and felt that it was joy.
> One song they sang, and it was audible,
> Most audible then when the fleshly ear,
> O'ercome by grosser prelude of that strain,
> Forgot its functions, and slept undisturb'd.
> (Prelude, II, 413–34)

Wordsworth felt, in his seventeenth year, all of nature 'work like a sea' and become a sympathetic mirror of his own inner being.

The language of this 'bliss ineffable' is distinctly Augustinian and is to be found not only here but in several other passages like it in *The Prelude*, and in 'Tintern Abbey'. It is the language of a progression toward revelation. The mind of the poet, spreading itself in sympathetic motion with all that lives and moves, passes over the sentimental immensity of the natural world that it might go beyond it, 'passing through all Nature', to rest with the inner revelation of the divine presence in the soul.

Augustine and Monica, during their conversation at Ostia, likewise pass over all things which give delight to the senses, and in this manner lay to rest the tumult of the flesh. Then in the silence of nature which ensues upon their having spoken of it, they move past it to make contact with the eternal wisdom. 'Our talk', St. Augustine writes,

had reached this point: that the greatest possible delights of our bodily senses, radiant as they might be with the brightest of corporeal light, could not be compared with the joys of that eternal life, could not, indeed even deserve a mention. Then, with our affections burning still more strongly toward the Selfsame, we raised ourselves higher and step by step passed over all material things, even the heaven itself from which sun and moon and stars shine down upon earth. And still we went upward, meditating and speaking and looking with wonder at your works, and we came to our own souls, and we went beyond our souls to reach that region of neverfailing plenty where *Thou feedest Israel* forever . . .

.   .   .   .

So we said: if to any man the tumult of the flesh were to grow silent, silent the images of earth and water and air, and the poles of heaven silent also; if the soul herself were to be silent and, by not thinking of self, were to transcend self; if all dreams and imagined revelations were silent, and every tongue, every sign; . . . and He Himself alone were to speak, not by their voice but in His own, and we were to hear His word, not through any tongue of flesh or voice of an angel or sound of thunder or difficult allegory, but that we might hear Him whom in all these things we love, might hear Him in Himself without them, just as a moment ago we two had, as it were, gone beyond ourselves and in a flash of thought had made contact with that eternal wisdom which abides above all things . . .[26]

[26] *The Confessions of St. Augustine*, trans. Rex Warner (New York and Scarborough, 1963), pp. 201-2.

In the silence of nature, by its exclusion from the inner recesses of the mind Augustine and Monica mount upward toward God. It is a journey made possible by the deliberate silencing of nature, by a willed muffling of the senses and of what is reported through them, even when it concerns God. A mediated form of communication with the eternal is supplanted by an immediate one.

So Wordsworth silences the song of nature that he might hear directly the music of the spheres of his own inner being. Wordsworth is able to travel inward in that visionary mood, rendered in Augustinian language, during his stay at Cambridge. By exclusion the forms of nature are made absent from his sight:

> And now it was, that, from such change entire
> And this first absence from those shapes sublime
> Wherewith I had been conversant, my mind
> Seem'd busier in itself than heretofore;
> At least, I more directly recognized
> My powers and habits: let me dare to speak
> A higher language, say that now I felt
> The strength and consolation which were mine.
> As if awaken'd, summon'd, rous'd, constrain'd,
> I look'd for universal things; perused
> The common countenance of earth and heaven;
> And, turning the mind in upon itself,
> Pored, watch'd, expected, listen'd; spread my thoughts
> And spread them with a wider creeping; felt
> Incumbencies more awful, visitings
> Of the Upholder of the tranquil Soul,
> Which underneath all passion lives secure
> A steadfast life. But peace! it is enough
> To notice that I was ascending now
> To such community with highest truth.
>
> (*Prelude*, III, 101–20)

Wordsworth pursues here a track 'not untrod before'.[27] In a clear repetition of St. Augustine's ruminating in the bowels of memory, 'the stomach of the mind', in Book X of *The Confessions*. Yet, where St. Augustine finds in the enormous reaches of memory the wonder of God, he does not find God; but Wordsworth discovers in the spreading power of his soul an intimation of its divine nature, of the 'Upholder' of it.

[27] *The Prelude*, III, 121.

Such visionary moments of the realization of the power of the
soul, and they are frequent in *The Prelude*, are followed by scenes
in which the face of nature is transformed. The soul, returning
from its inward journey, discovers in nature the theatre where its
power may be exercised. This is the case in the passage following
the mind's inward turning at Cambridge which I have just quoted:

> To every natural form, rock, fruit or flower,
> Even the loose stones that cover the high-way,
> I gave a moral life, I saw them feel,
> Or link'd them to some feeling: the great mass
> Lay bedded in a quickening soul, and all
> That I beheld respired with inward meaning.
>
> (*Prelude*, III, 124–9)

Meister Eckhart, on coming to himself after a vision of eternity,
saw in everything around him only God.[28] Wordsworth, having
turned inward from the silence of nature, discovers the awful
might of his soul, and upon returning possesses the conscious
awareness of the capacity of his mind to subordinate the forms of
nature to itself, to control the busy force of the senses. In the
aftermath of such moments Wordsworth realizes that he is both
'receiver' and 'creator' of what he sees; the mind of the poet is
divine in nature, and its creative interplay with the natural world
is a perpetual reminder to him of what he is—one of those higher
minds who, he discovers in meditation atop Mount Snowdon,

> . . . build up greatest things
> From least suggestions, ever on the watch,
> Willing to work and to be wrought upon,
> They need not extraordinary calls
> To rouze them, in a world of life they live,
> By sensible impressions not enthrall'd,
> But quicken'd, rouz'd, and made thereby more apt
> To hold communion with the invisible world.
> Such minds are truly from the Deity,
> For they are Powers; and hence the highest bliss
> That can be known is theirs, the consciousness
> Of whom they are habitually infused
> Through every image, and through every thought,
> And all impressions;
>
> (*Prelude*, XIII, 98–111)

[28] Ibid., II, 415–35. Here we can perceive a more dynamic sense of the mind's
auxiliar light.

The mood of exalted revelation upon Mount Snowdon is succeeded by a recollective meditation which constitutes its interpretation. The focus of this meditation is the scene which was revealed to the poet, but the condition that makes possible his reflection upon it is that it should no longer be present before him. It appears to him in memory, and its appearance is an image, 'The perfect image of the mighty Mind'. Contemplation of this image, given in revelation but becoming significant only in recollection, leads Wordsworth toward a stable and efficacious awareness of his poetic powers.

The image of the mind, whose horizon is articulated by the dynamic (but largely unspoken) interplay between the moon standing naked in the heavens and the 'blue chasm' where nature had 'lodg'd/The Soul, the Imagination of the whole', is the consummating figure in *The Prelude*. It has a steadying influence upon Wordsworth for it embodies the counterpoise between the inner world of the imagination and the framework of the natural mind which he so much desired as the condition that made the imagination efficacious. Such contemplation of the image of the mind does not lead toward a knowledge of the mysteries of its workings, but to a recognition of how its elements stand in relation to one another when there is a balance and harmony among them. In this recognition lay those calm moods when Wordsworth felt most himself, when, that is, his poetic powers were heightened, his very being was raised above the oppression of the senses.

We can get a clearer sense of just how such contemplation of an image could affect Wordsworth from his recurrent fascination with 'geometric science'. Geometry was for him an image of what was enduring and permanent in nature, and though his meditation upon the pure relations in the laws of nature did not lead him to a knowledge of their darker mysteries, he found a deeper pleasure in what this image of nature revealed to him of the powers of the mind:

> With Indian awe and wonder, ignorance
> Which even was cherish'd, did I meditate
> Upon the alliance of those simple, pure
> Proportions and relations with the frame
> And Laws of Nature, how they would become
> Herein a leader to the human mind,
> And made endeavors frequent to detect

> The process by dark guesses of my own.
> Yet from this source more frequently I drew
> A pleasure calm and deeper, a still sense
> Of permanent and universal sway
> And paramount endowment in the mind,
> An image not unworthy of the one
> Surpassing Life, which out of space and time,
> Nor touched by welterings of passion, is
> And hath the name of God.
>
> > (*Prelude*, VI, 142–57)

The charm of geometry for a mind 'beset/With images, and haunted by itself',[29] was precisely its power to lay to rest the tumult of the senses and free the inner powers of the mind. This power did not lie in the static image of a dynamic world which abstraction can articulate, but in the capacity of abstraction to convert the impure multiplicity of things in nature into an image of the mind's own power, and even, he suggests, of God. Contemplation of the image of nature, geometric and rational, leads not only to a freedom from intoxication with the busy dance of the senses, but, as well, to a heightening of the very being of the poet:

> I had been taught to reverence a Power
> That is the very quality and shape
> And image of right reason, that matures
> Her processes by steadfast laws, gives birth
> To no impatient or fallacious hopes,
> No heat of passion or excessive zeal,
> No vain conceits, provokes to no quick turns
> Of self-applauding intellect, but lifts
> The Being into magnanimity;
> Holds up before the mind, intoxicate
> With present objects and the busy dance
> Of things that pass away, a temperate shew
> Of objects that endure, . . .
>
> > (*Prelude*, XII, 24–36)

The contemplation of the image of nature as rational and geometric leads by a gradual progression to an intimation of the power of the mind. In his meditation during the night on Mount Snowdon Wordsworth confronts immediately the power of the

---

29 Ibid., VI, 179–80.

mind in the image of nature. The 'deep and gloomy breathing-place', through which mounts 'the homeless voice of waters', and the moon shining down upon the still ocean of mist 'In single glory', become the image of the power of a mind 'exalted by an underpresence/The sense of God, or whatsoe'er is dim/Or vast in its own being'. Through his meditation upon the vision induced by an exalted mood, the poet achieves a conscious awareness of the internal imaginative power of his mind and of the auxiliar light which flows from that awareness of inner power out upon the external world. This is, in Wordsworth's sense, imaginative revelation; the mind recognizes in the image of nature the figure of its own power over nature, the power to fashion from it 'A like existence' which will enable it to interpret itself to itself.

Comprehended in this manner, revelation (or apocalypse) is not something Wordsworth 'avoided'; he sought it, though it came most often unannounced, for in such moments of revelation he came to a conscious awareness of his powers as a poet. In this way Wordsworth was, he says, called back to his true self from an unfruitful and depressing entanglement in the passing shows of the present moment into which he had fallen through forgetful-ness of his real nature, and the authentic stewardship of his inner powers. Wordsworth's perception of his growth as a poet in *The Prelude* is built around two forms of self-forgetfulness. The first of these is the oblivion in which the child lives out its first days on earth; the second is the tyrannical dominance of the senses which leads, if not controlled, to a death of the inner being of the mind. Both conditions come from a lack of self-possession, the failure of the poet to be aware of his two natures and of the need to hold them in counterpoise to one another. Wordsworth found in the 'language of the sense', in the image of nature, the means to wield the elements of his mind, if not to understand them. In the image of 'A like existence' he found a means of achieving conscious self-possession of himself and his poetic powers, of maintaing a steady balance between the busy vortex of the senses and the abyss of his 'idealism'. Not that he could keep his balance for long. He was always, it seems, falling into a sensual self-forgetfulness from which he was summoned back in moments of imaginative revelation.

These moments occur throughout *The Prelude*. The crossing of the Simplon Pass is the most dramatic of these moments in which the power of the poet's mind is disclosed to him in an exalted mood, but it is not different in kind from the others. The writing of the passage in Book VI of *The Prelude* describing the crossing of the Simplon Pass is a form of meditation upon an image of nature leading progressively to a revelation of the mind's inner power. As at Cambridge, the mind turns inward upon itself and surveys the prospect of an image of nature constituted in the act of recollection. By surveying it, the mind passes beyond it toward a revelation of the great power underlying it, an 'unfathered vapour' from 'the mind's abyss'. Yet it is only from nature that the exalted mood of a visionary experience arises, and it is only in the image of nature, constituted by recollective meditation, that the mind of the poet finds the interpretation of its own inner power. The poet passes through the image of nature toward a revelation of the power of his mind, and then must pass back through it to find the language for interpreting the mind to itself.

[v]

In the poet's act of meditation upon the image of nature which leads him toward a recognition of the immense inner power of his mind, recollection is given a privileged position. For it is recollection which makes that recognition possible; in the transformation of nature into the image of nature the poet becomes conscious of his imaginative powers. The act of recollection forms the image which induces the poet's conscious awareness of the mind's inner freedom from the senses. In recollection the poet repeats the vision of the world he possessed as a child, the glory in a nature seen through the light of the anamnestic shadow still burning in the soul, and is able once again to exercise over nature the dominion of the child, to 'play' with it, to make of it the obedient servant of his will. This repetition, in an altered form, of the child's visionary experience is a form of recovery for the poet. It restores the 'virtue' of his imaginative freedom. Imaginative vision is not simply the anamnestic shadow of the mind cast upon nature, but the conscious recognition in recollection of the power of the mind over the 'outward sense'. The divine light of the soul wanes, the immortal spark fades, but the act of recollection keeps it alive, and it becomes the source of the mind's enduring strength. It is efficacious no longer through its presence, but through its absence, as a thing remembered.

The power of the imagination lies precisely in the distance the poet has come away from the anamnestic shadow of his childhood. In looking back upon the scene of his infancy, the sources of the poet's power open to him over the distance he has come and form a prospect in his mind. Yet when he comes close to them, altering the perspective of that prospect, they close before him as they were closed to him as a child. Only recollection of that experience brings it into consciousness, makes it signify to that awareness the mind's immortality and transforms it thereby into a source of imaginative power.

In the parabolic episodes which conclude Book XI of *The Prelude* we can see, if only partially (as is the case so often in Wordsworth), in what way recollection is privileged, how through it comes a recognition of the internal dominion of the mind over the 'outward sense'. The recollection of past moments, 'spots of time', restores the power of the mind when it is oppressed to depression by the weight and burden of the external world, and when it is exalted, raises it even higher:

> There are in our existence spots of time,
> Which with distinct pre-eminence retain
> A vivifying Virtue, whence, depress'd
> By false opinion and contentious thought,
> Or aught of heavier or more deadly weight,
> In trivial occupations, and the round
> Of ordinary intercourse, our minds
> Are nourished and invisibly repair'd,
> A virtue by which pleasure is enhanced
> That penetrates, enables us to mount
> When high, more high, and lifts us up when fallen.
> (*Prelude*, XI, 258–68)

What characterizes these moments, whose 'beneficent influence' reaches back 'As far as memory can look', is that from them the poet discovers the capacity of his mind to subordinate the senses:

> This efficacious spirit chiefly lurks
> Among those passages of life in which
> We have had deepest feeling that the mind
> Is lord and master, and that outward sense
> Is but the obedient servant of her will.
> Such moments worthy of all gratitude,

> Are scatter'd everywhere, taking their date
> From our first childhood: in our childhood even
> Perhaps are most conspicuous.
>
> (*Prelude,* XI, 269–77)

The two episodes which Wordsworth recounts, with the parabolic intent of making his point through them, are precisely moments when the mind seems not to feel itself to be 'lord and master' over the outward sense and finds in the place of mastery a 'visionary dreariness' investing the landscape.

In the first episode, Wordsworth recounts the story of a journey he took with a servant, 'honest James', on horseback across the moors at an age when he could scarcely manage the reins of the horse. He was separated from his 'encourager and guide', and, becoming afraid, dismounted and began leading his horse across the 'rough and stony Moor'. Lost, unable to control his horse while mounted, he stumbled on until he came to a bottom, where he found the name of a murderer engraved in the earth near the spot where he was hanged. Up to the point where he discovers the name of the murderer it is clear that in no way is the child master of his situation. But once he discovers the 'monumental writing' something curious happens:

> Faltering, and ignorant where I was, at length
> I chanc'd to espy those characters inscribed
> On the green sod: forthwith I left the spot
> And, reascending the bare Common, saw
> A naked Pool that lay beneath the hills,
> The Beacon on the summit, and more near,
> A Girl . . .
>
> (*Prelude,* XI, 300–6)

We are not told, and it seems not to be necessary to tell, why it is that upon seeing the engraved name in the earth he departs 'forthwith'. He ceases to falter, the bottom now gives on to a 'Common', and when he reaches the top of it he locates a pool, a beacon, and a woman. If he reascends the common, then he must have seen two of these things (at least), the pool and the beacon, before, yet it is only after he returns that they become significant for him. Each is mentioned twice in fifteen lines.

> It was, in truth,
> An ordinary sight; but I should need

Colours and words that are unknown to man
To paint the visionary dreariness
Which, while I look'd all around for my lost guide,
Did at that time invest the naked Pool,
The Beacon on the lonely Eminence,
The Woman, and her garments vex'd and toss'd
By the strong wind.
(*Prelude*, XI, 308–16)

Where before the child was faltering, lost, ignorant of where he was, it is now the guide who is invested with the adjective 'lost'. The child knows, it seems, where he is, or at least has the means to locate himself at hand; and, as in the second tale Wordsworth tells, where he waits, a feverish and restless schoolchild looking for the horse to come and take him home for Christmas, it is at the point where he begins to look for the absent guide that the landscape is invested with a visionary dreariness. In both tales the mind searches a landscape for what is absent from it, and does not find it. It is the presence of this absence (like Sartre's Pierre) that becomes the centre around which the scene constitutes itself. The pool, the beacon, and the woman become presences for him signifying the absence of his guide. This absence becomes manifest to him in the mood of dreariness which transforms an ordinary sight into a melancholy vision.

But it is not at this point that the recognition of the power of the mind to invest a scene with a mood comes; that is reserved for a later time, and it comes through the act of recollecting his experience there. The pretext for this is a second transformation of the scene. Later, Wordsworth tells us, 'in the blessed time of early love', when he visited

. . . this very scene,
Upon the naked pool and dreary crags,
And on the melancholy Beacon, fell
The spirit of pleasure and youth's golden gleam;
And think ye not with radiance more divine
From these remembrances, and from the power
They left behind?
(*Prelude*, XI, 320–6)

This too is simply, even abruptly, narrated, and again his concern is not with making clear how the scene itself was invested, but in

showing that it was transformed by such investment. And the
later transformation of the scene was affected by remembrance of
the earlier one, and made more powerful: 'So feeling comes in
aid/Of feeling'. Wordsworth discovers here the links binding one
feeling with another in an awareness of how each incrementally
affects the other. Yet that is not the point of this parabolic episode.
It comes in the next line: '. . . diversity of strength/Attends us, if
but once we have been strong'. (*Prelude*, XI, 327–8.) Feeling leads
to feeling, from earliest to latest, and back again to the earliest,
where the chain of feeling is discovered to have its base in some-
thing other than itself. The act of recollection leads Wordsworth
back to the scene of his infancy, and to the mystery of man that is
partially disclosed, yet mostly hidden, in his 'simple childhood':

> Oh! mystery of Man, from what a depth
> Proceed thy honours! I am lost, but see
> In simple childhood something of the base
> On which thy greatness stands, but this I feel,
> That from thyself it is that thou must give,
> Else never canst receive. The days gone by
> Come back upon me from the dawn almost
> Of life: the hiding-places of my power
> Seem open; I approach, and then they close;
> I see by glimpses now; when age comes on,
> May scarcely see at all, . . .
>
> (*Prelude*, XI, 329–39)

Recollection discovers in the scene of infancy, in simple child-
hood, an intimation of the base of the mind's inner power, of the
ground upon which the framework of the natural mind rests. Yet
the adult cannot repeat in recollection the experience of the sim-
plicity of childhood, for his being has become complex. But he can
recognize in it the source of his imaginative power, and from such
recognition comes a vivifying virtue for the mind, a virtue which
frees it from the oppression of the sense by granting it an aware-
ness of its divine nature. When Wordsworth draws close, in
recollection, to the source of his power, it closes off before him. It
is no longer open before him, it is lost; but its virtue is not, for it
becomes efficacious when he recognizes it as the origin of his
power, a power which is constituted in the act of recollection. It is
no longer present in the simplicity of the child, but has come to

reside in the complex activity of the adult's consciousness, where in memory it abides, though altered. This is, for the poet, the meaning of growing up; the experience in nature of the divine power of the mind is transformed in recollection into its own meaning, and that meaning as a presence in memory becomes the source of the poet's power, becomes, that is, the imagination.

CHAPTER IV

Archimedes' Machine

[1]

IN *The Cyberiad* Stanislaw Lem, the Polish master-storyteller nar-
rates a fable about a machine which the 'constructor' Trurl put
together that could make anything starting with the letter *n*.
Trurl grew very excited over the powers of his machine, and in his
excitement overpraised its abilities to his friend Klapaucius to
such a degree that Klapaucius became annoyed and asked if he
might test the machine's skill himself.

'Be my guest', said Trurl. 'But it has to start with *n*.'
'*N*?' said Klapaucius. 'All right, let it make Nature.'
The machine whined, and in a trice Trurl's front yard was packed
with naturalists. They argued, each publishing heavy volumes, which
the others tore to pieces; in the distance one could see flaming pyres,
on which martyrs to Nature were sizzling; there was thunder, and
strange mushroom-shaped columns of smoke rose up; everyone talked
at once, no one listened, and there were all sorts of memoranda,
appeals, subpoenas, and other documents, while off to the side sat a few
old men, feverishly scribbling on scraps of paper.
'Not bad, eh?' said Trurl with pride. 'Nature to a T, admit it!'[1]

Klapaucius is not satisfied that what the machine has made is
nature; he feels that the machine not quite fairly got the better of
him. But aroused now to the contest of wits with it, he does not
pause to quibble, and proceeds to think up other tests for his
friend's machine.

But we must pause here in Klapaucius's place, for Trurl's
machine, in creating a nature that is a thing residing in books,
memoranda, and scraps of paper, has posed for us in a single figure
the problem we face in discovering what Wordsworth meant when
he spoke in the 'Preface to the Excursion' of the 'marriage' of 'the
discerning intellect of Man' to 'this goodly universe'. His poem

---

[1] Stanislaw Lem, 'How the World was Saved', *The Cyberiad*, *Fables for the Cybernetic
Age*, trans. Michael Kandel (New York, 1976), pp. 9–10.

was to be the 'spousal verse' of that 'great consummation'. In it the union of mind and external world was to be enacted and proclaimed to 'arouse the sensual from their sleep/Of Death'. This 'marriage' was to be consummated on paper first, and then made known to the world at large, a 'star-like' presence, 'Shedding benignant influence'. The mind of man, which is the 'main region' of his song, and nature come to reside together in the book which Wordsworth makes; their union is for him the image of poetry.

In Wordsworth's poetry nature is that which rises up over against man as other than himeslf, but only within a sphere which man has already circumscribed. It stands, as Shelley similarly maintained in 'A Defence of Poetry', before man as the necessary reflector of the mind without which the mind would be empty, deprived of the image of itself. Yet for Shelley all things exist only in so far as they are perceived, and, thus, the mind becomes the creator of its own reflector. We find a similar circumscription of nature stated in a more elaborate philosophical language in the *Biographia Literaria*:

> Bearing then this in mind, that intelligence is a self-developement, not a quality supervening to a substance, we may abstract from all *degree*, and for the purpose of philosophic construction reduce it to *kind*, under the idea of an indestructible power with two opposite and counteracting forces, which by a metaphor borrowed from astronomy, we may call the centrifugal and centripetal forces. The intelligence in the one tends to *objectize* itself, and in the other to *know* itself the object.[2]

What the mind 'objectizes' becomes the object through which the mind comes to know itself as it develops. This self-development of the intelligence is a process inherent in a nature which comes to know itself in and through the mind of man. For both Shelley and Coleridge the nature which finds its place in their poetry is not a thing separate from the mind of the poet, but a being constituted by the mind and posited by it as its means of interpreting itself to itself. The interplay of mind and nature is grounded upon the play of the mind with its own images, both of itself and of nature. Wordsworth's intention in the 'Preface' was to 'describe the Mind and Man/Contemplating' in conjunction with 'the Thing/Contemplated'.

[2] S. T. Coleridge, *Biographia Literaria,* ed. J. Shawcross (Oxford, 1967), vol. I, p. 188.

The image of the union of mind and nature in Wordsworth's poetry is invoked by a perception of how exquisitely they are seemingly fitted to one another. This reciprocal fitness of one for the other appears, in the 'Preface to The Excursion', as the ground of their union, a union in which the mind is united with its external opposite. It is a presupposition of the 'Preface' that the fitness of inner and outer worlds is a pre-established, but concealed, matter which it is the task of the poet to disclose and allow to stand as the 'simple produce of the common day'. The relation of fitness between these worlds finds its ground, presumably, in a conception of a totality which forms the basis for the articulation of the space of transcendence between them. Yet in Wordsworth's poetry of the imagination there is no clear conception of totality, only an intimation of its presence, which, coming in an exalted mood, leads inward toward an apperception of the inner power of the mind, and not outward toward a vision of the world as a system. This apperception of the inner freedom of the mind is equated more than once by Wordsworth with revelation. From such revelation there arises, in the act of recollecting the experience of an exalted mood, a sense of a totality dimly apprehended through the workings of the poet's mind. God and man, Wordsworth says in *The Prelude*, divide between them the 'great system of the world'.[3] Wordsworth appropriates as the 'main region' of his song the mind of man, and leaves to God, as it were, what remains of the great system of things. In choosing the mind of man Wordsworth obtained the basis from which a vision of this system, of nature and the God who animates it, was possible. He found that from the mind of man came an intimation of the world as a totality circumscribing finite and infinite, mortal and immortal, mind and nature: for in the image of this totality he discovered the immortal nature of his soul.

There is in Wordsworth's poetry an interplay between mind and nature which is expressed as a narrative of the mind's coming to a conscious discovery of its powers. Nature is the medium, the language of this discovery, and is, consequently, not essentially an external presence to the mind, but, rather, something circumscribed by it already, before it is converted into the language of the mind's self-discovery. It is the relationship between an already circumscribed nature and the narrative structure of Wordsworth's

[3] *The Prelude*, XIII, 267.

poetry of the imagination that I wish to work out in this chapter; to try to see how nature comes to reside in the poem enacting its union with the mind.

The immediate link for Wordsworth between mind and nature is the senses. Through them man acquires a voice for the inner silence of the mind. He becomes present to himself in the presence of the other which is not himself. Were it not, Emerson says in his great essay 'Nature', for the existence of rocks, trees, streams, and birds, our inner being would be unknown to us. The language of the sense is the 'anchor' of Wordsworth's soul. In nature he finds reflected the image of his creative mind, as he discovered atop Mount Snowdon during a meditation upon the vast field of mist lying open to the eye of memory between the moon and the abyss from which rose the sound of waters. He becomes conscious in this recollective meditation of the character of his own powers of mind. The scene which is significant for the eye of memory had no such meaning when it was immediately and spontaneously perceived. It is the image of the scene, not the scene itself which becomes important to Wordsworth.

Meaning is not spontaneously present in the scene which takes Wordsworth by surprise as he ascends Snowdon, but emerges into consciousness through the processes of a subsequent meditation upon it. It is a situation where the poet sits down beside what happened before him, turns his back on it, as it were, in order to discover its meaning. He must, to put it in temporal terms, place the events occurring in the present moment into the past before they can appear as significant for him. Without the intervention of such recollective meditation the mind and its image would belong to a single sphere within which they would remain undifferentiated. This state of absolute reflexivity, where inner and outer worlds form a single prospect within the mind, would resemble an experience Wordsworth described earlier in *The Prelude*:

> Oft in these moments such a holy calm
> Did overspread my soul, that I forgot
> That I had bodily eyes, and what I saw
> Appear'd like something in myself, a dream,
> A prospect in my mind.
>
> (*Prelude*, II, 367–71)

In elevated moods, when mind and nature become a single prospect, there is an absence of meaning, a silence into which both the mind and nature sink. Recollection of them is for Wordsworth a discovery of their meaning that enables the mind to become conscious of its inner powers in a separation from nature, a separation in which the mind grasps itself as master over the senses. This awareness of mastery coincides with the meaning of what is disclosed in the recollection of the exalted mood in which mind and nature form a single prospect. Mastery over the senses does not come immediately from the experience of such a mood, but is achieved through the act of recollection in which the meaning of that mood is disclosed.

In the Fenwick note to the 'Intimations Ode' Wordsworth described his early experiences of the external world. It was for him an insubstantial presence not readily distinguishable from the active spirit within him. Accompanying this experience was a feeling that he would not die, but be translated to heaven like Elijah:

I used to brood over the stories of Enoch and Elijah, and almost persuade myself that, whatever might become of others, I should be translated, in something of the same way, to heaven. With a feeling congenial to this, I was often unable to think of external things as having external existence, and I communed with all that I saw as something not apart from, but inherent in, my own immaterial nature.[4]

The infant's perception of the world as 'vanishings' and 'Fallings from us' occurs outside time, in the absence of a temporal sequence. In those moments of an exalted mood when external and internal worlds become indistinguishable time is also absent, and the return from them is accompanied by a recovered, often keener, temporal awareness. And the ascent up Snowdown ends in a vision of the eternal and infinite mind; the final step of that journey, the reflexive encounter of the mind and its image, carries Wordsworth out of time. These three moments are not identical, though their relation to one another is very close. They differ first in the degree to which is present a conscious apprehension of the meaning of the relationship between mind and nature; and, second, in the way in which the act of recollection itself has intervened and determined the meaning of that relationship.

In each of these moments, which can be roughly perceived as stages in the irregular progression of the mind of the poet toward

[4] *PW.*, vol. IV, p. 463.

a conscious self-possession of his imaginative powers, there is an intense interplay between the inner freedom of the mind and the structure of the natural mind that is finally articulated in the act of recollection. How this occurs can be comprehended through the relation established between the temporal sequences of sensible nature and the atemporal perception of a totality immanent in the mind. The relationship between the eternal inner being of the mind and its finite nature is articulated through an experience of the spontaneity of the present moment and its interpretation in recollection. If we turn first to 'Tintern Abbey' we can discover, I think, the terms which will enable us to comprehend the relation of mind to nature as it is represented in the three moments I have indicated.

[II]

'Tintern Abbey' turns about the event of conversion in which the experience of the present moment as a reviving memory becomes itself a memory of the present moment. The revival of the 'picture of the mind' as the poet reposes 'under this dark sycamore' and gazes upon the landscape of the 'sylvan Wye' is accompanied by conscious recognitions of what is seen once again, but as well by the awareness of 'somewhat of a sad perplexity'. It is from the act of recognition that the poet's perplexity arises, for, in reviving, the scene residing in memory confronted by its external, actual counterpart discloses to him the distance he has travelled from it; he learns that he has altered inwardly, that he has lost something that was once his in the presence of the landscape now before him. This landscape was once an 'appetite' for him, 'That had no need of a remoter charm,/By thought supplied, nor any interest/Unborrowed from the eye'. Now, with the time of 'thoughtless youth' past, nature is no longer the immediate object of the eye and ear, but has, even as he stands in its presence, a 'remoter charm' arising from his self-conscious recognition in recollection of a scene he once experienced unselfconsciously. Both experiences of the landscape are absorbed into a future that will be essentially the same as the past. The present moment, manifest in the gaze directed at the scene from under the dark sycamore, is absorbed homogeneously by the recollection of the past and its projection into a future which is essentially identical with it, as in 'The Tuft of Primroses' where memory and hope are made one.

The appetitite of the 'thoughtless youth', which found satisfaction in devouring the immediately present shapes and colours of nature, becomes in time the 'pleasing thoughts' of the adult; these find in the present moment from which the poem arises, 'life and food/For future years'. The 'present pleasure' he experiences is different from the 'former pleasures' he reads in Dorothy's eyes; his eyes are no longer 'wild' as hers are, but calm and meditative, and made powerful through the mood induced by the harmony and joy they perceive. What he sees in the landscape, though it is present, is already remote, distanced from him by the act of recognition confiscating the immediate experience of the landscape and converting it, upon the basis of his past experience, into a hope for the future. It is a landscape perceived from a physically removed station, for what is seen in it is blurred and indistinct; this distance is repeated in the act of recognition. The memory of the landscape of the Wye becomes itself a means for the poet to distance himself, even when absent from the present scene, from the oppression of the immediate moment. The landscape remembered in bitter times in the city is a restorative; it is a source of freedom from the harshness of life, not that it enables him to escape it, but that it prevents him from succumbing to it.

This distance is only one of many which constitute the essential form relationships assume in the poem. The poet's recognition of a long absence from the Wye constitutes itself through the long perspective of the scene before him. What he perceives forms a totality of earth and sky, water and wood, unified by the station from which he has chosen to view it. This distance is repeated temporally as a distancing, and ultimately as an elision of the present moment through its conversion into a past which is regarded as essentially identical with a future that is not about to be, but already is present. But its presence is shaped by recollection; in the turn backward toward what he has been the figure of what he will be is construed. Whether the poet turns in spirit to the absent Wye, or to the scene present before him, the effect is the same; the presence of what is seen is confiscated by recollection and given a place in the 'mansion' of memory.

It is a landscape remembered that he perceives before him, a 'picture of the mind' reviving. His present perception of it is different from his earlier appetitive apprehension of it; he feels it as more remote. Having indicated the process through which the landscape is restored for him, Wordsworth then turns to a description of his earlier, more thoughtless, yet more immediate experience of nature. In the distance covered in this narrative description, the 'dizzy raptures' of his youth are transformed into the sustained, but subdued passion of a constant lover of 'all that we behold/From this green earth'. To make this journey is, however, to suffer loss, and for what is lost, the appetitive craving for immediate pleasure in the things of nature, the poet finds 'abundant recompense', or so he 'would believe'. He has learned, he says, to regard nature differently from the way he saw her in his youth when she was 'all in all' to him. Now his relation to her is more remote, more controlled, for nature no longer constitutes an all-encompassing totality, but is seen mediately through the borrowed charm lent by the 'still, sad music of humanity', and by the felt presence of something which circumscribes nature:

> And I felt
> A presence that disturbs me with the joy
> Of elevated thoughts; a sense sublime
> Of something far more deeply interfused,
> Whose dwelling is the light of setting suns,
> And the round ocean and the living air,
> And the blue sky, and in the mind of man:
> A motion and a spirit, that impels
> All thinking things, all objects of all thought,
> And rolls through all things.

In perceiving nature and the 'language of the sense' as finite elements of an embracing totality whose presence is felt through them, but is felt as something which lies beyond them as well, Wordsworth distances himself from nature, and though he sees in nature the 'anchor' of his 'purest thoughts', the chain linking him to it is amply long. Nature is a thing recollected, a resident in memory's house. And in recollecting nature he achieves that 'blessed mood',

> In which the burthen of the mystery,
> In which the heavy and weary weight
> Of all this unintelligible world,
> Is lightened:—that serene and blessed mood,

In which the affections gently lead us on,—
Until, the breath of this corporeal frame
And even the motion of our human blood
Almost suspended, we are laid asleep
In body, and become a living soul:
While with an eye made quiet by the power
Of harmony, and the deep power of joy,
We see into the life of things.

Turning inward upon the landscape of the mind leads the poet toward his purest thoughts, but the gift of this mood does not come directly from nature, it comes from the image of nature formed in recollection.

In the last movement of the poem, where the poet turns to his 'dearest Friend', and finds in the 'shooting lights' of her 'wild eyes' what he once was, we find the clearest and most completely sustained passage from the immediate experience of nature to nature recollected. The distances here are several, and they are complexly related to one another. The poet reads in her eyes what he once was; he hears in her voice the language of his 'former heart' and knows that she will never succumb, because of this, to the 'dreary intercourse of daily life'. He then foresees a time when she too shall change, as he did, and the wild ecstasies of the present moment will come to dwell in her memory, and the living presence of nature shall reside in her recollection. And going beyond that, foreseeing his own death, he looks toward a time when he himself would be absent from everything except her memory. In the concluding lines of the poem the poet stands before a landscape present to him as a thing recognized through recollection, which is bound to a past and a future essentially identical with one another, but then separates himself even further from this moment by another act of recollection which *might* occur in some future time, and attributes this act to his companion. This displaced recollection of a nature recollected, is the final articulation of a poem intending the absorption of the present moment into memory. Memory is for the poet the source of his power, and it is efficacious only in the absence of the pressure of the present moment.

The act of recollection becomes possible at the moment when nature ceases to be all in all in an immediate and spontaneous experience, and mediation begins. The recollection of what nature is (or was) is articulated as a narrative about a time past and not repeatable, yet recoverable to a degree in memory. Such recovery becomes a self-reflexive narrative, a story told about itself. The narrative springs up from a loss of immediacy which finds 'abundant recompense' in recollection. It does not in any adequate way account for the sad perplexity which comes from recognition once again of the reviving picture of the mind; nor does it explain how that loss occurs, how he has changed, but rather tells that he has changed. The conversion of this loss, through recollective recognition of it, into a narrative manifests a belief ('I would believe') in which loss is converted into gain. It is a belief, a story told, which bridges the distance between past and future opened up by the sense of loss and perplexity found in the experience of the present moment. Without this narrative bridge the past would be an experience isolated from the present by an awareness that one cannot go back, that in the passage of time a change occurs which makes the past unrepeatable. If the past were only an isolated element in a consciousness that could see in it, by comparison with the present, only its diminution, then the future would offer a terrible vision of a life steadily worn down by loss to transparency and evanescence. It would possess an insubstantiality unbearable for consciousness.

But when loss is then converted into gain, through a narrative arising from a recollection of that loss, we see that the story told is about the power of memory itself. In memory what is lost when nature ceases to be an immediate appetitive object is converted into a restorative power; into, that is, a higher form of seeing, where 'all which we behold/Is full of blessings'. In a nature apprehended purely by the senses, where the present moment is privileged over the others, the life of things is seen; it is a 'feeling and a love' for colour and form. But in the mood rising out of the remembrance of an absent nature it becomes possible to 'see into the life of things'.

It is in the present moment where loss occurs, where time passes, and the mystery of change conceals itself. And it is in memory that change and loss first become manifest. Without memory there would be no sense of loss. Without the present moment there would be no loss. Wordsworth converts the oppositional tension between memory and the present moment into a narrative told about what will happen to his companion whose presence in the 'now' of the poem is seen as a figure embodying his past existence. It is a narrative similar in structure and import to the one he has told of himself in which she too will undergo the loss of her spontaneous rapture in the presence of nature. This loss will become in time, so the story goes, the 'mansion for all lovely forms', where nature will dwell, no longer an immediate joy, but a recollected pleasure. The present moment is elided, and the mystery of change concealed within it is now doubly hidden. Past and future are as one, a permanent structure into which the present is admitted as a disguised inhabitant, as either a restorative from the past or a hope for the future.

But Wordsworth does not halt his narrative when he has converted the present wildness of his companion's eyes into his past, and her future into his present. He goes on from there to transform his present into a past which will reside, in the future, in her memory:

> Nor, perchance—
> If I should be where I no more can hear
> Thy voice, nor catch from thy wild eyes these gleams
> Of past existence—wilt thou then forget
> That on the banks of this delightful stream
> We stood together; and that I, so long
> A worshipper of Nature, hither came
> Unwearied in that service: rather say
> With warmer love—oh! with far deeper zeal
> Of holier love. Nor wilt thou then forget
> That after many wanderings, many years
> Of absence, these steep woods and lofty cliffs,
> And this green pastoral landscape, were to me
> More dear, both for themselves and for thy sake!

The poet will become a resident 'worshipper of Nature' in the mansion of her memory. The figure of the poet gazing upon the landscape before him is absorbed by this future act of recollection; he comes to have a place in the narrative which rises out of the act of recollection inspired by Dorothy's presence. Not only does the poet's act of recollection absorb the presence of the present moment in the poem into the mansion of memory, but this very act of recollection itself is absorbed by a future act of recollection. With this final act of recollection the present moment is elided from the poem. This last recollective movement repeats the one preceding it, where the present moment becomes a disguis resident in the dwelling-place of memory. In the recollection of an act of recollection the nature of recollection is concealed from itself. Recollection as it becomes the mansion of memory serves to conceal the present moment as a source of loss; the act of recollection is an act of concealment eliding the present, and in recollecting itself conceals from itself its own concealing nature.

The landscape of the Wye is dear to the poet both for its own sake and for that of his companion. Its presence is transformed for him into memory, a past which is also a future, and in the act of future recollection attributed to his companion by his narrative, his presence in the immediate moment of the poem is elided, as something belonging to the present moment which threatens discontinuity and loss, and concealed in the narrative identity of past and future. The poet is hidden by his own narrative, and remains twice removed from the presence of the scene before him which he felt to be the source of his poem. Like an Indian fakir, the poet climbs up the rope of his poem and disappears into the mansion of memory. The landscape of the Wye is a source whose presence, as something immediately present, is perpetually concealed from him. The mansion of memory is not a static structure, but an act continually repeated in which the present moment, concealing within itself the mystery of change and loss, is hidden, and is transformed, on the basis of that recollective concealment, into a narrative of recompense, where what is lost is more than amply restored.

[III]

The conversion in 'Tintern Abbey' of the experience of the present moment (as a source of loss) into a narrative of loss and recompense through recollection gives to us the movement by which nature is circumscribed and brought into a text, but it does not make clear in what way it enables the poet to articulate by its mediation the relation of mind and nature celebrated as a marriage in the 'Preface to The Excursion'. Our understanding of this union can be made more precise, I think, if we regard it through the perspective offered by the three different moments of its irregular development already indicated, the last of which, the vision atop Snowdon, presents a form of consummation. The other two, one taken from the 'Intimations Ode' and Wordsworth's commentary in the Fenwick note upon it, and the other from Book II of *The Prelude*, can be seen, roughly, as moments in an irregular progression toward that consummation.

In the 'Preface to The Excursion' Wordsworth chose the mind of man as his 'haunt', the main locus of his song; in the Fenwick note to the 'Intimations Ode' he specifies the 'region' of the poem as the world of his own mind. It was his aspiration, he says, to make use of the notion of the pre-existence of our souls as an Archimedean point upon which he might rest the machine that would enable him to manœuvre the elements of his own mind:

Archimedes said that he could move the world if he had a point whereon to rest his machine. Who has not felt the same aspirations as regards the world of his own mind? Having to wield some of its elements when I was impelled to write this Poem on the 'Immortality of the Soul', I took hold of the notion of pre-existence as having sufficient foundation in humanity for authorizing me to make for my purpose the best use of it I could as a Poet.[5]

Wordsworth's concern for where the poem should 'rest' is repeated earlier in the same note when he refers specifically 'to particular feelings or *experiences* of my own mind on which the structure of the poem partly rests'.[6] Archimedes wanted a point outside the earth, from which he might move it. The point upon which Wordsworth rests his own machine is not the traditional notion of pre-existence; from that he receives only the authority for using his own 'notion' of pre-existence. The traditional concept does not allow him to stand outside the world of his own mind, but it does give him an impetus toward stepping outside it on his own terms. The world he moves outside of is not the one constituted by the present condition of his mind, but the world of the mind of the child, a world 'not realized'. This is the world the adult has fallen outside of into a much different place. The 'machine' Wordsworth employs to wield its elements is the act of recollection; by it his former world is moved into a reciprocal and beneficent relation with his present one:

> O joy! that in our embers
> Is something that doth live,
> That nature yet remembers

5 Ibid., p. 464.
6 Ibid., p. 463.

What was so fugitive!
The thought of our past years in me doth breed
Perpetual benediction . . .

As we have seen in other chapters, it is the adult's act of recollection which discloses the significance of the child's anamnestic experience of the world. In the discovery of the divine nature of that experience, the poet finds ample recompense for the loss of the experience itself. He possesses its meaning, and such possession is a joyous remembrance, for in it the past becomes an intimation of the future, informing its meaning. But if it is recollection that serves as Wordsworth's Archimedean machine for moving the world of his mind, it is also from recollection that the notion of pre-existence comes. This notion serves as the point from which he may wield the elements of his mind. The machine, in effect, rests upon itself, and this may go some way in explaining Wordsworth's concern over exactly where it should rest.

In the 'Intimations Ode' the world of the child is constituted through, and wielded by two recollections. Wordsworth indicates these in a letter to Mrs Clarkson: 'The poem rests entirely upon two recollections of childhood, one that of a splendour in the objects of sense which is passed away, and the other an indisposition to bend to the law of death as applying to our particular case.'[7] In the Fenwick note Wordsworth elaborates upon the relation between the child's perception of things in nature 'Apparelled in celestial light', and the sensation of its own immortality. This sensation manifests itself in the act of perception, which is for the child both a source of fascination and a trap into which he falls:

But it was not so much from [feelings] of animal vivacity that *my* difficulty came as from a sense of the indomitableness of the spirit within me. . . . I communed with all that I saw as something not apart from, but inherent in, my own immaterial nature. Many times while going to school have I grasped at a wall or tree to recall myself from this abyss of idealism to the reality. At that time I was afraid of such processes. In later periods of life I have deplored, as we have all reason to do, a subjugation of an opposite character, and have rejoiced over the remembrances . . .[8]

Objects are invested with a 'dream-like vividness and splendour' when, as inherent participants, they become part of the activity of

---

[7] Ibid., p. 464.
[8] Ibid., p. 463.

the child's indomitable spirit, pieces in the game he plays with his world, fragments 'from his dream of human life'. What the child sees participates directly in the life of his mind; it is not seen *as* inhering in the mind. It is inseparable from the mind. The distinction implied by Wordsworth's *as* is a later intrusion upon the experience by the remembrance of it. The child's perception of the external world *as* internal is accompanied by a feeling 'congenial' to it: an inability to sense his mortality. When at the outset of the 'Intimations Ode' the natural world is seen as external and separate from the mind, the poet discovers in this act of perception that he has undergone an internal alteration. The visionary gleam has vanished, and the world outside him now speaks immediately to him of what he has lost. It is a manifest presence of what is no longer there. What he does recognize from the way things appear to him is his own mortality; where once he was unable to sense his own mortality as he moved about in a world of visionary radiance, he now, in losing that splendour, gains sight of his own mortality. From the finite perspective of the latter world he looks back upon time past, and, in recollecting it, converts the loss he feels immediately in the present moment into a source of recompense for what is lost, which unifies memory and hope, past and future. The present moment, as a source of loss, is once again elided.

The basis of this recompense is recollection, which is rendered here, as we saw in detail earlier, as the narrative of the journey of the soul/star through the land of the dead. The soul/star which sets in heaven rises upon earth, and, according to the logic of the narrative, when it sets on earth it will rise in the skies of its heavenly home. At one time blinded to his mortality by an anamnestic shadow of surpassing radiance, then at another seeing only his mortality in a universe of death illuminated by the fading light of his inner being, the poet, in eliding the present moment which speaks only death and loss to him, comes to reside in a world constituted by recollection, dominated by the narrative of memory, where mortality and immortality, radiant shadow and the light of common day belong to a single totality. Within this totality each element leads into its opposite, and back again— immortality to mortality, mortality to immortality. The mind of the poet, whose elements Wordsworth aspires to wield through the machinery of recollection, remains sovereign. The threatening aspect of the present moment, which could throw into chaos the world of the mind, is concealed, and a balance of sorts is struck between the indomitable spirit dwelling in the mind of the poet and the power of the senses to speak only loss to that mind. The mind, which comes into possession of its inner powers through the act of recollection, resists the subjugation which the senses threaten. This remembrance, over which Wordsworth rejoiced, having lost his fear of the 'abyss of idealism' and its processes within his mind, is a form of recall, by whose means the poet comes to himself in recalling the image of himself.

[IV]

In Book II of *The Prelude* Wordsworth records a moment from his early youth, when, sitting alone 'upon some jutting eminence' at sunrise, he gazes over the quiet valley below. As he looks down upon his world in silence and solitude, a calmness overtakes him, and, held in the spell of the exalted mood induced by it, he perceives the world as a presence once more inherent in his mind:

> . . . and before the vernal thrush
> Was audible, among the hills I sate
> Alone, upon some jutting eminence
> At the first hour of morning, when the Vale
> Lay quiet in an utter solitude.
> How shall I trace the history, where seek
> The origin of what I then have felt?
> Oft in these moments such a holy calm
> Did overspread my soul, that I forgot
> That I had bodily eyes, and what I saw
> Appear'd like something in myself, . . .
> (*Prelude*, II, 360–70)

The motifs found in the child's anamnestic vision of the world in the 'Intimations Ode' are repeated in this moment: the world is perceived as from a great height; and as a thing inherent in the mind. Though it remains unspoken here, the valley touched by the rising sun has become a field of light, a scene invested with a glory and radiance very like that which illuminated the world inhering in the mind of the infant.

Yet Wordsworth neither describes this illumination nor names its source. Both are unspoken, as is, it would seem, the place of this record in his narrative. For though it occurs within a field of light, at sunrise, it is a dark moment for his powers of recollection, leading him to question his ability to trace out his intended history: 'How shall I trace the history, where seek/The origin . . .?' What had begun earlier, with the image of the 'infant Babe' (*Prelude*, II, 237), as a narrative description of the growth of his natural mind, 'a register/Of permanent relations' (311–12) comes up against a mode of feeling with no 'origin' in nature, and no place in his narrative register. This feeling is 'a trouble' (291) come into his mind 'From unknown causes' (292). Left to himself at the death of his mother, he finds that his mind of itself remains open to the 'influxes' of nature which form in the framework of the natural mind a comprehensive and comprehensible structure of images. These images form a ground for an experience of nature in which there are no images:

> . . . and hence, from the same source
> Sublimer joy; for I would walk alone,
> In storm and tempest, or in starlight nights
> Beneath the quiet Heavens; and, at that time,
> Have felt whate'er there is of power in sound
> To breathe an elevated mood, by form
> Or image unprofaned; and I would stand,
> Beneath some rock, listening to sounds that are
> The ghostly language of the ancient earth,
> Or make their dim abode in distant winds.
> Thence did I drink the visionary power.
>
> (*Prelude*, II, 320–30)

The scene in which the landscape becomes a prospect in his mind is intended as a counterpart to this one, where the power of tranquility is presented as equally efficacious as that of grandeur and tumult. The latter scene induces in him a fleeting mood of 'shadowy exultation', but remains firmly a part of the interplay of the presence and absence of images within an external nature, where the power embodied in the sound of the wind invokes a kindred power in his 'purer mind'. It is a fleeting moment of exultation whose real power is not immediately manifest, but emerges in its remembrance:

I deem not profitless these fleeting moods
Of shadowy exultation: not for this,
That they are kindred to our purer mind
And intellectual life; but that the soul,
Remembering how she felt, but what she felt
Remembering not, retains an obscure sense
Of possible sublimity, to which,
With growing faculties she doth aspire,
With faculties still growing, feeling still
That whatsoever point they gain, they still
Have something to pursue.
                            (*Prelude*, II, 331–41)

What is gained in such recollection of what is not remembered is
not a knowledge of what is felt, but from how the soul felt comes
an intimation of the soul's infinitude, a sense that no matter how
large and intricate the framework of the natural mind grows to be
the inner reaches of the mind will remain free, will never be con-
fiscated by the sensual faculties. This inner awareness of the soul's
freedom, of something 'evermore about to be', is the acquisition
of recollection, and it leads toward the completion of the narrative
register which Wordsworth is recording, and to the Poet's con-
scious self-possession of his imaginative powers.

The narrative register which Wordsworth records here is a
form of double entry bookkeeping, a diptych in which the fleeting
moods induced by the sublimer aspects of nature are to find their
counterpart in scenes of calm tranquillity leading likewise, in their
'wise passiveness', to a similar conscious possession of the mind's
power. But in the moments when inner and outer worlds become
one world inhering in the mind, the poet seeking the same source
of 'sublimer joy'as in the grander scenes of nature, suddenly finds
himself baffled, unable any longer to find the origin of his mood
in nature, or within himself. The narrative breaks off, and another,
concerning the modifying power of the mind over nature begins.
What is absent here is (and it is seen as a privation both of the
present moment of the experience and for the act of recollection
turned upon it) an emergent image bodying forth, like Venus
rising from the sea,[9] the process by which the mind becomes
aware of its power. Wordsworth comes close to what he recog-

---

[9] Cf. *The Prelude*, IV, 102–5: 'I have been busy with the toil of verse,/Great pains
and little progress, and at once/Some fair enchanting image in my mind/Rose up,
full-form'd like Venus from the sea.'

nizes is unspeakable for him, and allows it to remain unspoken. This is not the case with his visionary experience on Snowdon.

[v]

What most distinguishes the 1805 version of the ascent of Snowdon·from that appearing in the edition of 1850 is the description of the 'blue chasm' fracturing the ocean of mist stretching out before the poet and usurping the landscape. The difference between them is important, for in the later version the lines locating the 'Imagination of the whole' within that fissure in the mist are elided. This would seem to imply, and it has been so taken by many of its interpreters, that in the later repetition of the earlier description the locus of the imagination has been shifted from the abyss upward to the moon hanging fixed and isolated in the clear sky. And accordingly the emphasis in interpreting these passages has fallen more upon the modifying function of the imagination, than upon determining the relationship between it and the 'underpresence' that exalts the mind, and from which comes the recognition of the mind's absolute inner freedom. This scene, intended in both versions as an emblem of the union of mind and nature, seems to present to the mind meditating upon it an embodiment, for the senses, of the principal act of the imagination and of the source of its agency in the mind. What dominates in Wordsworth's representation of his meditation upon the image of a 'mighty mind' is the description of the excursive power of the mind. Yet, in the 1805 version, the links connecting the mind feeding upon infinity with its modifying power over nature remain unarticulated. What unites the act and process of the imagination with its source stays, it would seem, hidden.

The excursive power of the mind, in both descriptions of it, leads through its activity toward a recognition of the mind's inner, divine nature:

> Such minds are truly from the Deity,
> For they are Powers; and hence the highest bliss
> That can be known is theirs, the consciousness
> Of whom they are habitually infused
> Through every image, and through every thought,
> And all impressions; . . .

> (*Prelude*, XIII, 106–11)

From the modifying activity of the mind Wordsworth becomes conscious of the powers of the imagination. And this activity appears here as the source of his awareness of the mind's internal freedom. Such recognition and self-awareness seem to proceed immediately from the action of the mind upon the external world and upon its inner reaches.

But the mind's recognition of its power in its excursive and modifying action is not in itself an emergent awareness of its 'transcendent power'. A more primary recognition of transcendent power precedes and informs what the mind discovers of its inner nature in thrusting itself upon the external world. A capacity of the mind to modify its perceptions of things does not entail, taken in itself, a recognition of the mind's divine power; but once that power has been disclosed, then the modifying activity of the mind can be perceived as coming from it as an embodiment of its freedom from nature. It is here that the importance becomes clear of the elision of the lines in the 1805 *Prelude* locating the 'Imagination of the whole' in the dark abyss from which rises the sound of waters. In the elided lines the imagination is localized as a source, and is related, but not clearly, in Wordsworth's meditation upon his vision, to a sense of what is dim and vast within the mind. It appears as a fixed breathing-place from which rises the excursive power of the imagination.

In 1850 repetition of the description of this vision and the meditation upon it, the sound of waters rises from the abyss, but the imagination is not located in it, nor is it situated in the emblem of the moon. The moon 'broods' over the abyss. It is an act, and from that act comes a recognition of the mind's transcendent power:

> When into air had partially dissolved
> That vision, given to spirits of the night
> And three chance human wanderers, in calm thought
> Reflected, it appeared to me the type
> Of a majestic intellect, its acts
> And its possessions, what it has and craves,
> What in itself it is, and would become.
> There I behold the emblem of a mind
> That feeds upon infinity, that broods
> Over the dark abyss, intent to hear
> Its voices issuing forth to silent light

In one continuous stream; a mind sustained
By recognitions of transcendent power,
In sense conducting to ideal form,
In soul of more than mortal privilege.

(Prelude, 1850, XIV, 63–77)

The image of a mind given us in the 1805 *Prelude* renders manifest
what is dim and vast within it and exhibits its highest function,
without making equally manifest their relationship. It is an image
of the mind directly informed by the spontaneous immediacy of a
vision recollected, and is grounded upon the figure of the mind's
act of directly perceiving the natural scene presented to it.

The image of a mind represented in the 1850 version is grounded
differently. The moon brooding over its dark abyss, intent on the
voices issuing from it, bears little resemblance to the act of
directly perceiving an external scene. Rather it represents the mind
meditating on a scene recollected, and from this act of meditative
recollection comes a recognition of the mind's transcendent
power, and this in turn informs and determines the character of the
mind's excursive power and the self-awareness it produces. From
the mind inwardly turned upon itself in recollective meditation on
an image of nature comes a recognition of the inner transcendent
vastness and infinitude of the mind. In this act of recognition the
imaginative power of the mind is constituted.

It is not from the immediate vision of a natural scene that the
recollective recognition constituting the fundamental character of
the imagination comes, but from the image of that scene remem-
bered, over which the mind broods. The immediacy of the vision
embedded in the present moment is elided. The excursive power
of the imagination over the spontaneity of the present arises from
the act of recollective recognition of the mind's power to modify
it.

The modifying power of the imagination does not proceed
from a fixed source in either the mind or nature. It comes from the
act of recognition in recollection, and it has no source of which
the poet can speak, for this act is what brings what is new into the
world and cannot, therefore, be accounted for by anything which
preceded it. This act of the mind is made manifest, but not intelli-
gible, by the image of a natural scene recollected. It remains unin-
telligible for Wordsworth, yet the image of the mind coming from
the image of nature induces in him a mood in which he comes to

an awareness of its power, and this awareness enables him to wield that power as a poet. From this act of the mind, which in itself is transient, uncaused, and fundamentally discontinuous, arises a narrative of the growth of the mind towards a stable awareness of itself. The discontinuity of the mind becomes in the narrative told of it a stable and stabilizing presence from which the continuity of a life emerges. Yet it is a continuity which does not circumscribe or coincide with its discontinuous matrix. Rather the mind seeks continually to exclude its own random discontinuity.

The narrative arising from the mind's recollective meditation upon its own image constitutes a foundation for the continuity of the growth of the mind toward an awareness of its inner powers. The mind which has once come into conscious possession of its powers through the image of them taken from nature is able to convert in retrospect the discontinuity of its development into a narrative of the discovery of itself. It is an idiosyncratic narrative, Wordsworth says, which all men are condemned to tell of themselves, for each man is a memory unto himself. The language of this narrative comes from the mind's experience of nature, its union with it; this union is consummated in the act of recollection and from it proceeds the transcendent freedom of the mind before the natural world, a freedom Wordsworth identified with the highest powers of the imagination.

Index